New Life in the Neighborhood

Abingdon Press   **Nashville**

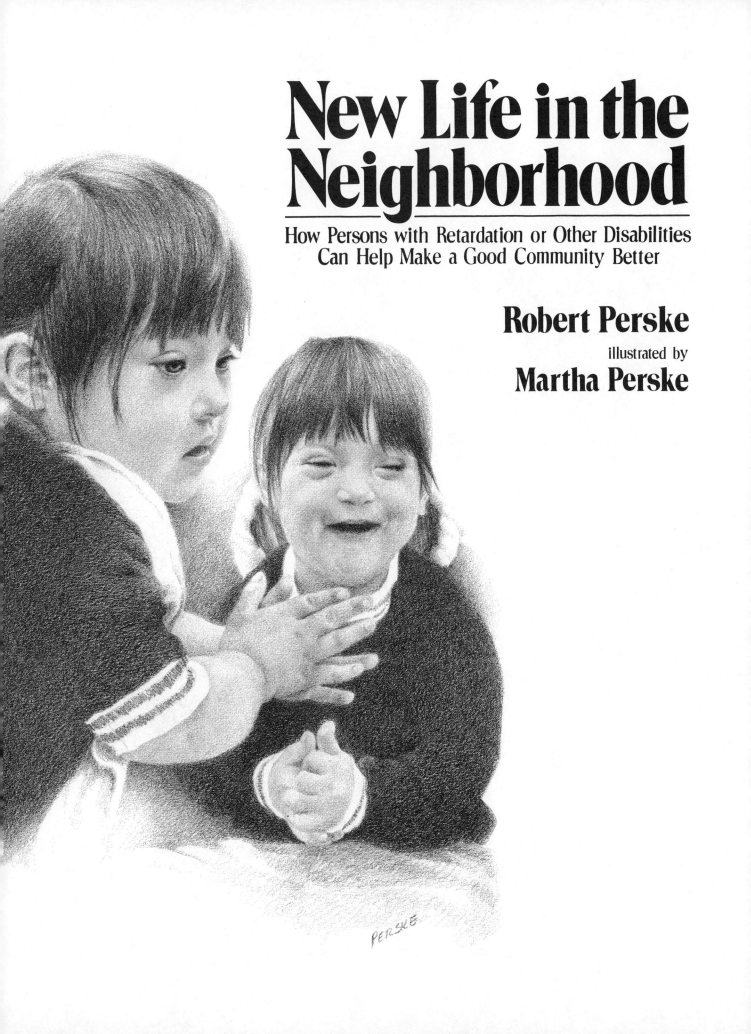

New Life in the Neighborhood

How Persons with Retardation or Other Disabilities
Can Help Make a Good Community Better

Robert Perske

illustrated by
Martha Perske

New Life in the Neighborhood

Copyright © 1980 by Robert and Martha Perske

Tenth Printing 1991

Library of Congress Cataloging in Publication Data

PERSKE, ROBERT. New life in the neighborhood.
  1. Developmentally disabled—United States.
  2. Developmentally disabled—Care and treatment—
United States. I. Perske, Martha. II. Title.

HV3006.A4P47   362.1'968'0973   80-15517

ISBN 0-687-27800-7

Contents

PERSKE

1
The Reason
for This Book

• It is as if civilization has put on a better pair of glasses. Our society is making radical changes in the way it views persons with mental retardation, cerebral palsy, autism, epilepsy, learning disabilities, and other developmental disabilities. For hundreds of years those persons were seen as an embarrassment and as hindrances to our progress, and most were sent away to live in institutions. Then beginning in the 1950s, a remarkable chain of discoveries led society to begin to correct its perceptions and to see such people as *valuable, individual human beings,* who—except for extreme medical and educational problems—never should have left their neighborhoods in the first place.

• As a result of this perceptual revolution, these once devalued and segregated persons are moving back into their own communities throughout the United States and Canada. And to our surprise, their presence, more often than not, has added zest and rejuvenation to the neighborhoods in which they are living.

• Of course, in a few communities there have been headline-making objections to the return of persons with handicaps, but most communities are welcoming them quietly, as they would any new neighbor. Usually there are no fanfares, or press conferences, or celebrities cutting ribbons stretched across front porches. Instead, there are the usual Hello-I-live-next-door and Let-me-know-if-you-need-anything statements, and that's all . . . at first.

• Now you have become interested in people with developmental disabilities—at least enough to be holding this book in your hands. Good! Read on. If people with handicaps have moved into your community—or if you wish some would—this book is definitely for you. It describes

> *new discoveries* (which may lead you to see people with handicaps in a new way);
> *new ways neighbors are relating* (which may start you thinking about creative relationships you could develop);
> *fresh ideas about improving our civilization* (which can emerge from successful two-way relationships between you and people with handicaps).

• Hearing about neighborly relationships with people having developmental disabilities pricked my curiosity so much that my tape recorder and I found ways to become guests in many small, well-run, familylike residences for these persons in both Canada and the United States. But my interest did not stop there. I began visiting ordinary citizens who live close to such homes. And the more I listened to them, the more I felt the need to share their thoughts with people like you.

• So here goes—and here's hoping this book is helpful to you.

Within the past three years, I have been lucky enough to gather extra tapes and notes while traveling about the continent on writing assignments and activities with
• Random House, Inc. (search for "cutting edge" concepts with persons having severe and profound handicaps, funded by U.S. Government Developmental Disabilities Office Contract No. HEW-105-76-5001);
• Association for Retarded Citizens—National Headquarters (activities as a member of its National Residential Services Committee and special assignments with the committee chairwoman, Eleanor Elkin);
• The Association for the Severely Handicapped (collaboration leading to the publication of R. Perske; A. Clifton; B. McLean; and J. Stein, eds., *Mealtimes for Severely and Profoundly Handicapped Persons* [Baltimore: University Park Press, 1977]);
• The President's Committee on Mental Retardation (preparation of the Report to the President, *Mental Retardation: The Leading Edge—Service Programs That Work* [Washington, D.C.: PCMR, 1978]);
• Canadian Association for the Mentally Retarded (writing of *Listen Please,* a special edition of *Deficience Mentale/Mental Retardation* [Toronto: CAMR, 1979]).
Then came the ultimate good fortune when the President's Committee on Mental Retardation—especially Fred Krause and Allen Menefee—afforded me the opportunity to interview 158 people who live close to 87 familylike residences, each containing six or fewer persons with handicaps.

2
People Who Face an Obstacle Course

Some people who are different are moving into neighborhoods throughout the United States and Canada, and I want to help you really get to know them.

Some have problems with their speech, but that does not mean they do not want to talk to you.

Others have limbs that do not always cooperate, and they will need to use braces, crutches, or wheelchairs in order to go places with you.

Like you, they have inner urges to improve themselves. However, when you are confronted with a certain task, you may tackle it like a soaring seagull, while they have to work like birds with short wings to accomplish the same feat. Even then, some will not make it, because the goal is simply beyond their reach.

Many have physical disfigurements, and at first glance you may think them unattractive; you may even be repulsed. However, when you get to know them, you may find such deep human beauty and zest that it will make you feel good just to be with them.

They, too, feel hurt and humor, but you may not sense these emotions right away. Society has programmed you to build a wall between yourself and such people so that you can hide from their feelings. Then if and when you take down your wall, you may find another wall—theirs. And only after they are sure you will not belittle or hurt them will they consider letting this second wall come down.

A few may have strange-looking seizures, and others may make bizarre movements with their hands, heads, or bodies. But even actions like these now can be understood. For example, the fish that suddenly races at high speed, wiggling and ramming into other fish, may be regarded as weird by the other creatures in the sea. But they may not see the hook in its mouth, or the line attached to it. Today as never before, we can understand the "hooks" that are present in the lives of the people with handicaps who reside in our neighborhoods.

These people can be your neighbors now because, not so very long ago, the public hit upon a fresh way to view persons with handicaps. It discovered that:

These people are like you and me in every way except one—They have a *developmental disability*.

I will explain. Each of us came into this world as a small bundle, containing thousands of developmental forces. Each tiny component, like a single musician in a gigantic symphony orchestra, was designed to do its part at the right time. Together, those forces triggered the enlarging, strengthening, and deepening that enabled you and me to change from tiny babies into mature adults within approximately twenty-two years.

Most of us moved through this masterpiece of growth with comparative ease, but a small number did not. Somewhere, somehow, and usually with no warning, a few of us seemed to have a monkey wrench thrown into our developing systems. A chromosome became broken or lost its way; an invading parasite interfered; a foreign substance upset the chemical balance; or a physical blow disturbed some of the workings. Of course, when this happened, many different people moved in as fast as they could to adjust the system and get it back on track. However, there simply was not enough knowledge and skill to repair it completely—or help just did not get to the scene fast enough.

Afterward, development was never again as easy or as automatic for those of us who incurred such disabilities; it became like an obstacle course, *and we were destined to work for the rest of our lives to overcome or to live with the wounds caused while we were growing up.*

Of course, such explanations describe tragedies that we hope someday will be eliminated. But until that happens, all is not lost. For example, neighbors like you can *understand* what happened to these people. You can *visualize* the obstacles they must face in life. And when they make gains, you can *recognize* the hard work and heroism it required. Knowledge like this can start you caring about what happens to these people with handicaps. It can even move you to quietly cheer them on.

On the other hand, I shudder when I think of the explanations for such handicaps that we professionals would have given you no more than twenty years ago—and the fright such explanations would have provoked in you. We have come a long way in our thinking since then!

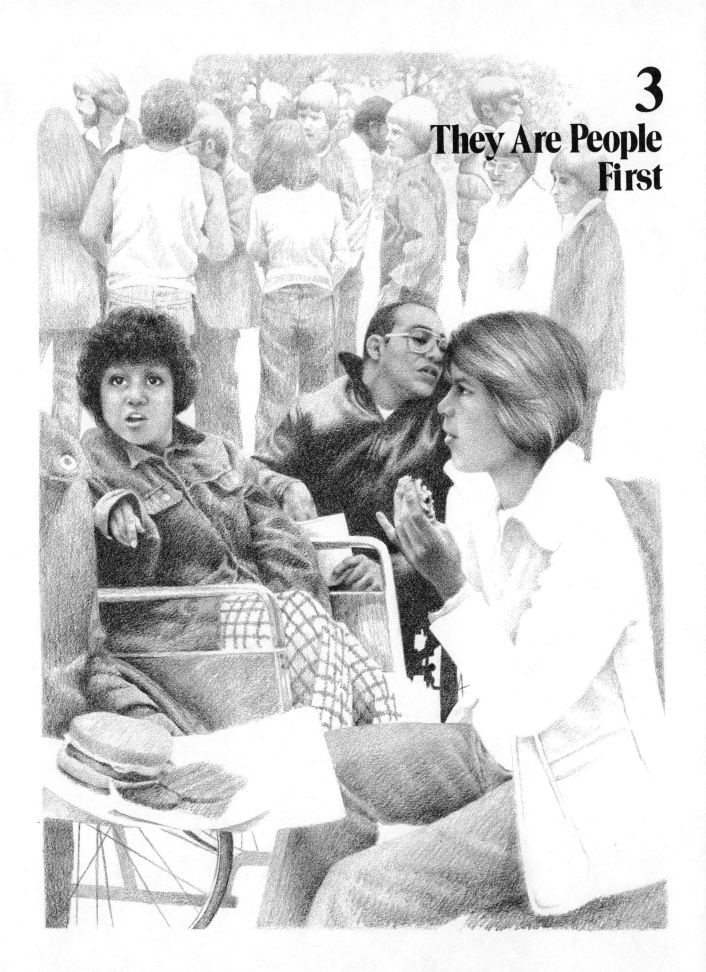

3
They Are People
First

Not many years ago, we did not know very much about developmental disabilities, but we were outstanding in the way we labeled and classified people who had them. People were called

mentally retarded
cerebral palsied
epileptic
quadriplegic
deaf-blind
autistic.

Some even more esoteric and mysterious sounding classifications were

mongoloid
gargoyle
cretin

and many more terms that need not be listed.

Of course, diagnostic labels like these were created by professionals in order to identify the various types of handicaps. And in all fairness, it should be said that many of those professionals are laboring over another such process now. With a new sensitivity, many are trying to make sure that diagnostic labels do not belittle or demean those who receive them. For example, some clinicians have developed a policy of using a label only as a noun referring to a condition (e.g. *a person with mental retardation*). Very infrequently do they allow a label to be used as a noun referring to a person (e.g. *the mentally retarded* or *the retardate*), or even as an adjective (e.g. *the mentally retarded person*).

But the worst effects of professionally created labeling are manifested in the conversation of ordinary citizens. You might hear a person on the street say, "What's the matter with that Johnson fellow?" And another would answer, "He's a mongoloid." Then the two would nod and give each other deep knowing looks *as if they knew everything* about the man—when in most cases, neither of them would even know what the word mongoloid means.

When ordinary citizens speak in that way about people with handicaps, it is as if they were pinning large badges on them. The diagnostic words on the badges draw so much attention that everyone around the poor labelees becomes blind to their attractive qualities. Such a practice is cruel, belittling, and unfair.

Today, it is the persons with handicaps themselves who are pleading most against insensate and unfair labeling practices. For example, a group of former residents of the Fairview State Hospital and Training Center in Salem, Oregon, had been struggling to choose a name for their innovative new self-advocacy organization. During the debate, a young woman rose to speak. She said, "We are tired of being seen as retarded. We want to be seen as people, first!" After this sincere, plaintive plea, the group was inspired to drop the other suggestions and name their organization People First. A most poetic choice. That young woman expressed the deepest longing of thousands of people with handicaps who lived even before she was born and who had hated being called retarded but could not do anything about it. Today, People First organizations are springing up throughout Canada and the United States, and that woman's plea will be repeated by thousands.[1]

The United States government responded to that plea, and on November 6, 1978, Public Law 95-602 was signed, *abandoning the use of categorical labels in defining persons with developmental disabilities*. It focused instead on the actual barriers that stand in the way of normal development. The law states that any person having substantial impairments in at least three of these seven precious functions of everyday living is in need of special understanding and help from the government.

1. self-care
2. receptive and expressive language
3. learning
4. mobility
5. self-direction

---

1. The forms of address suggested by some forward-thinking professionals and the plea of the woman from Salem have influenced me to construct the sentences of this book so that the words *persons, people, citizens,* and *human beings* appear first and the words for their *handicapping condition,* second.

6. capacity for independent living
7. economic sufficiency

In this law, persons with developmental disabilities definitely are being seen as people first.

But the most hopeful result stems from the fact that many neighbors like you are viewing these people in that way, too. For example, Maggie Roggerio in Los Angeles was asked why she repeatedly held parties at her house for the men and women with handicaps who lived next door (these celebrations will be described in more detail later). She replied, "It's fun having parties with these people. . . . People—I guess that's the key. I see them as people before anything else."

So with what we now know, you have rich opportunities to look for beauty and value and talents in such persons, before focusing on their handicaps. In fact, you can become so good at this searching that if someone asked you, "What's the matter with that Johnson fellow?" you would not resort to the simple, mindless statement, "He's a mongoloid." Instead, it would be possible for you to respond with a sincere, thoughtful description of his attractive characteristics first, and later to tell of the barriers you have been watching him tackle in his struggle to grow and develop.

4

The Enlightening Principle of Normalization

Sometimes new knowledge can stimulate people to do things they never have done before. For example, when people believed the earth was flat, their laws and their living were conditioned by a dread fear that those who traveled too far would drop off the edge. Then a few intrepid souls dared to sail beyond those mythical limits, and they returned. When the bits of new information they brought back were pieced together, it dawned on humankind that the earth was round! This single principle inspired people of all professions and occupations to explore new directions too numerous to mention in one book—or even in one library— and the world was better for it.

A remarkable concept called the *principle of normalization* has inspired the field of developmental disabilities in that way. It has illuminated hundreds of nooks and crannies that heretofore had been dark and shady. It has cast fresh light on all our dealings with persons having such handicaps. As a result, the quality of living for these persons has begun to rise as never before in the history of the world.

The new ideas grew out of Denmark's sweeping reforms of 1959. And the first notion was probably conceived by N. E. Bank-Mikkelsen, the director of the Danish Mental Retardation Service. According to reports, he, in this new mission, "began to compare what he saw in the lives of residents of institutions with what he saw in his own life. He thought of the comforts he enjoyed, such as sofas and stuffed chairs, spacious and colorful rooms, a private bedroom and bath. He thought of his stylish clothes and his television set. He could find no justifiable reason for the disparity, and he began to search for a better alternative."[1]

As a result, he developed the "concept of normalized settings," which he described as "letting the mentally retarded obtain an existence as close to the normal as possible."

Other Scandinavian countries were moved by Denmark's bold step, and two Swedish leaders, Karl Grunewald and Bengt Nirje, came up with a refined definition: "Making available to all mentally retarded people patterns of life and conditions of everyday living which are as close as possible to the regular circumstances and ways of life of their society."[2]

In the meantime, Gunnar and Rosemary Dybwad, international experts from the United States, who are without a doubt the field's most traveled persons, began to call attention, as they lectured and consulted throughout the world, to what was happening in Scandinavia.

Then an American, Wolf Wolfensberger, proposed a technical definition: "Utilization of means which are as culturally normative as possible, in order to establish and/or maintain personal behaviors and characteristics which are as culturally normative as possible."[3]

So there you have them—three different attempts to explain the principle in a few words. Feel free to pick the one that defines it best for you.

But attempting to define completely all aspects of the principle has been like trying to catch a sunbeam in the hand—something always escapes. The Swedish leader Nirje, who is also a poet, probably has captured many of its rays:

Normalization means . . . *a normal rhythm of the day*.
You get out of bed in the morning, even if you are profoundly retarded and physically handicapped;
you get dressed,
and leave the house for school or work, you don't stay home;
in the morning you anticipate events,
in the evening you think back on what you have accomplished;
the day is not a monotonous 24 hours with every minute endless.
You eat at normal times of the day and in a normal fashion;

---

1. State of California Health and Welfare Agency, *Way to Go* (Baltimore: University Park Press, 1978).
2. R. Kugel, and W. Wolfensberger, *Changing Patterns in Residential Services for the Mentally Retarded* (Washington, D.C: President's Committee on Mental Retardation, 1969).
3. W. Wolfensberger; B. Nirje; S. Olshansky; R. Perske; and P. Roos, *The Principle of Normalization in Human Services* (Toronto: National Institute on Mental Retardation, 1972).

not just with a spoon, unless you are an infant;
not in bed, but at a table;
not early in the afternoon for the convenience of the
staff.

Normalization means . . . *a normal rhythm of the
week*.
You live in one place,
go to work in another,
and participate in leisure activities in yet another.
You anticipate leisure activities on weekends,
and look forward to getting back to school
or work on Monday.

Normalization means . . . *a normal rhythm of the
year*.
A vacation to break the routines of the year.
Seasonal changes bring with them a variety of
types of food, work, cultural events, sports,
leisure activities.
Just think . . . we thrive on these seasonal changes.

Normalization means . . . *normal developmental
experiences of the life cycle*.
In childhood, children, but not adults, go to
summer camps.
In adolescence one is interested in grooming,
hairstyles, music, boyfriends and girlfriends.
In adulthood, life is filled with work and responsibilities.
In old age, one has memories to look back on, and
can enjoy the wisdom of experience.

Normalization means . . . *having a range of
choices, wishes, and desires respected and
considered*.
Adults have the freedom to decide
where they would like to live,
what kind of job they would like to have, and can
best perform.
Whether they would prefer to go bowling with a
group,
instead of staying home to watch television.

Normalization means . . . *living in a world made of
two sexes*.
Children and adults both develop relationships
with members of the opposite sex.
Teenagers become interested in having boyfriends
and girlfriends.
And adults may fall in love, and decide to marry.

Normalization means . . . *the right to normal
economic standards*.

All of us have basic financial privileges and
responsibilities,
are able to take advantage of compensatory
economic security means, such as child allow-
ances, old age pensions, and minimum wage
regulations.
We should have money to decide how to spend; on
personal luxuries or necessities.

Normalization means . . . *living in normal housing
in a normal neighborhood*.
Not in a large facility with 20, 50, 100 other people
because you are retarded.
And not isolated from the rest of the community.
Normal locations and normal size homes will give
residents better opportunities for successful
integration with their communities.[4]

Although the normalization principle is extremely positive, its strongest function lies in its
power to uncover conditions and practices which
for centuries had *denormalized* people with
handicaps, and to which little attention had been
paid. Here are only a few examples of the way it
used to be:

getting up at 5 A.M. and being dressed and fed before
the 7 A.M. change of shift;
going to bed early for the convenience of the staff;
being seen as one of a group and never as an
individual;
eating, sleeping, recreating, and working, within
the same walled-in area;
wearing "community" clothing;
spending mealtimes in large, noisy, odoriferous
dining rooms;
or being fed while lying on your back in bed;
being forced to eat rapidly in order to adhere to a
group schedule;
never being in a room by yourself;
always feeling you are a few notches below the staff
and wishing you were as good or as privileged as
they are;
working in the laundry for a dollar a week;
receiving payments in coupons because you aren't
trusted with money;
being told by the chaplain that if you mind the aides
and work hard, you'll get out some day;
knowing that most professionals keep looking for
your sickness and your badness, instead of
pointing out your strong points;

---

4. Canadian Association for the Mentally Retarded, *Orientation Manual on Mental Retardation* (Toronto: National Institute on Mental
Retardation, 1977).

seldom being allowed to decide anything for yourself;

being deprived of a public school education even though your family pays taxes for such a "compulsory" education;

suffering the low expectations of those around you when you try anything new;

seldom or never interacting with persons in regular communities;

existing in a setting apart from those of the opposite sex;

never riding in a staff person's private car because of institutional rules;

repetitiously eating the same government-issue picnic food—hot dogs, baked beans, potato chips, and Kool-aid;

sitting for long hours in "day rooms," with no programs;

traveling in buses with the institution's name painted on the sides;

being expected to die young;

and then being buried in the institution's cemetery with your patient number, instead of your name, on the tombstone.

Until the principle of normalized settings arrived on the scene, those of us working with persons with developmental disabilities often didn't know any better than to treat them as we did. But we sometimes shudder when we think of the past. And we will be happy to leave it all behind as something historians will ponder, at some future date.

Notice, however, that the principle does not argue for *the normalization of people*. We never could agree upon the definition of "normal." It calls for *normalized environments,* which are more nurturing to persons with handicaps than the artificial, out-of-the-way environments that were created in the past.

But one of the most enlightening facts coming out of the principle may have to do with you and with where you live. It may help you to see clearly that the most normalized environment for some persons with handicaps is your own neighborhood.

If you randomly picked ten persons, and if you learned how they reached their present stage of development, you might discover an interesting fact: Each of the ten would have an internal *blueprint* and *rate of development* distinctly different from the others. (Of course, environment would be a factor, too, but that will be considered later.)

If I were one of the ten, you would learn that once I wanted to be like Joe DiMaggio, the great baseball player. But it didn't take long for me to find that I did not have his blueprint and rate of growth, especially when it came to hitting fast-moving balls with a bat. Later, I wanted to be like theologian/philosopher Paul Tillich. But I did not have the brains that he had, so his blueprint and rate obviously were different from mine, too. Finally, I learned that my highest dignity and greatest joy in living came not from trying to be what others were, but from developing into the best Bob Perske I could be, with the unique strengths and weaknesses that I possess.

It is my hunch that within you there is a story like mine. And the same could be said for Albert Einstein, the scientist; Margaret Mead, the anthropologist; Biff Capone, the policeman; or Sabrina Woytzic, the waitress. Such a view raises some interesting points.

Although each of us is shaping up differently, all of us are still developing. This can be seen when someone tells us that we cannot do a certain task. That usually makes us work harder to prove that we *can* do what our detractor says we cannot. Sometimes—to our surprise—we are successful. And when that happens, we feel simply great; at other times, however, we fail. Nevertheless, *we had the chance to try*.

Until recently, persons with developmental disabilities were not given the same chances to develop that we were given. The professionals in charge of their care predicted what they could or could not learn. Then they were forced to live within the limits that had been prophesied. Of course this was not done with malicious intent; many professionals of earlier days simply were not aware that there was a better way.

Today, we find that when persons with handicaps are given the same freedom and support to develop that we have, they often surprise us. Peter Graves, a helper in an auto body shop, is one of these persons.

• Peter Graves was sent to an institution in 1949 after a diagnosis of *Mental Retardation: Encephalopathy due to Postnatal Cerebral Infection*. Since he was not expected to develop normally, he stayed at the institution for 25 years, with the government paying a total of $432,600 for his keep. Of course the later years were the most expensive: The government paid $21,624 for 1974, his last year.

• However, by 1979, Peter Graves had been living in his hometown for five years, and he
—was working full-time in the auto body shop;
—had moved from a small-group home into his own apartment;
—no longer received supplementary income checks from the government;
—recorded a taxable income of $11,752.85 for 1978;
—paid $1,620 in income tax to the government;
—received only periodic follow-up counseling from a regional caseworker (average cost to the government: $17 per month).

Other things about Graves' developing life may not show up in monetary figures, but they are just as valid. For example, his eyes brightened during an interview when he described how a mangled auto fender can be reshaped, ground down, hot-and-cold shrunk, plastic-filled, puttied, sealed, sanded, and painted. He spoke warmly about his three-year working relationship with Robert Swanlund, his boss: "Bob says I'm comin' and I am. A good body-man's gotta have a good eye and steady hands—and Bob says I'm gettin' 'em." It was learned from Swanlund that during the "blizzard of '78," when auto and bus traffic was snarled, his employee walked two miles through driving snow to get to work. On another day, he came to work with a fever of 103° and had to be returned to his apartment and put to bed. It is obvious that the current Peter Graves—the worker and the man—is far from the kind of person he was prior to 1974.

The success of this former resident of an institution was encouraged by Bob Swanlund's exciting discovery that Peter Graves was a developing person, too. And it was this single notion that energized the productive relationship that followed.

Many neighbors of persons with handicaps in all the states and provinces are catching the same spark. They are learning that it doesn't take much effort to observe the measurable development that these persons are struggling to achieve. It takes a bit of watching and listening—and sometimes it means asking a few questions of those who are working with the person.

Does my friend have an individual program plan?
What specific goals is my friend working on now?
How are people helping him to accomplish these goals?
How often do you review my friend's progress?

More often than not, you will find that those who work with your friend will be thrilled that you asked. And it is altogether possible that the answers you receive will be so interesting that you will be moved to ask one more important question: *Is there something I can do to help my friend meet these goals?* Most workers will respond to this question as if it were music to their ears. Usually, they need all the help they can get.

I have seen neighbors take great interest in watching people with handicaps achieve goals that have to do with

sucking from a straw
controlling tongue movements
rolling over
crawling
walking
holding a spoon
getting dressed
recognizing safety signs
counting money
shopping
riding a bus
worshiping in a church or synagogue
developing proper manners
sitting with a friend who is ill
being regular on a job
living alone in an apartment.

And when you begin watching the measurable progress of your neighbor that closely—let's face it! You could "get hooked" on the fact that your friend is just as developmental—according to his or her own blueprint and rate of growth—as the rest of us. Then you may begin to wonder why you were not aware of it before.

Old Repulsions Are Fading

"I'm going to do the best I can when we get to that church, because if I don't, *that building will go away*." That's a strange perception, but that's the way eleven-year-old Marie Vaccaro saw it in 1958, when she and fourteen other residents from an institution traveled to an experimental Saturday special-education program in a midwestern community church. Ever since Marie had been committed to the institution five years earlier by a judge who "found her to be mentally retarded," in her spunky way she had been trying all sorts of methods to shield herself from the full force of that wounding repulsion. And somehow, in this vivacious young girl's mind, it was less painful for her to believe that buildings—and people—literally were moving away from her, than to think that any entity, human or not, would totally eject her from the community where she had started to grow up.

Even so, Marie never knew about the awkward discussions with the church board and how the church janitor became angry because a classroom "would be used by *those* kids when everything needs to be kept spotless for Sunday." Also, none of the fifteen special-education-students-for-a-day knew that when the board finally approved the use of a classroom, they issued a stern admonition to those of us who had volunteered as faculty. "Since children like this are known to be unkempt, you are being held responsible to see that the classroom is left exactly as you found it." The way it was said did sting a bit. Nevertheless, we agreed to comply. It was the last request, however, that hurt most. "We want you to bring your students into the church by the alley entrance."

In that situation, we the faculty—who were seen as upstarts for bringing people back into a community that had sent them away—had to answer softly every attempt to repulse our boys and girls. But really, since it was 1958, that church board was to be commended for even listening to us. After all, we had tried to get the same precious fifteen youngsters into the YMCA swimming program that same year and had received a flat no, because the YMCA administrator was convinced beyond a doubt that the children would urinate in the pool.

These happenings were only minute slices of the massive mountain of repulsions that persons with developmental disabilities were accustomed to receiving from almost every corner of the community. Without any objective investigation or judgment, these persons were rejected as if they were

possessed by evil forces
carriers of "bad blood"
a drag on the community's resources
the products of illicit sex
subhuman organisms
too ugly to be seen in public
persons to be laughed at
a minority that would outbreed us
people with dread sicknesses
sexual monsters and perverts.

A few citizens in some communities did claim that these special people were emissaries from God and had come among us to give us a particular message or to test our compassion. However, even that belief didn't put a stop to the pervasive repulsion that existed at one time.

In those days, you and I were *conditioned* to feel uncomfortable around such people. Somehow, our parents and our teachers, by what they said (or didn't say), very subtly *programmed* us to believe that if we got too close to people like that, whatever evil they had would rub off on us.

This terrible prejudice came about because persons with developmental disabilities offended our society at the point where it was most vulnerable: *We worshiped the idea that we were becoming better and better*! And everyone was expected ultimately to develop

a pure heart
a brilliant mind
a beautiful body
a successful marriage
a high status job—or a beautiful home
and live in a perfect society.

Then along came this tiny number of defenseless persons with obvious physical and mental handicaps. Their presence challenged our fondest dreams—and they had to go.

Of course, the labels were the clinchers. Earlier, the diagnoses would have read *feeble-*

minded, moron, idiot, or *imbecile.* (It is hard to believe that words like these were once created in clinics.) Later, the labels were those mentioned in the preceding chapters. And more often than not, when the people were labeled, they became classified in the same manner as carrots, chairs, or pieces of limestone, making it impossible for them to be seen as persons at all.

Since *nonpersons* were not expected to be capable of hurt, humor, or love, it was easier to send them out of the community to live in institutions. When that happened, the repulsion was complete, and we could get on with our business of making a perfect world.

However, there are three issues which, in all fairness, need to be clarified.

- In earlier years, a few families did refuse to send their sons and daughters with handicaps to institutions, and they kept them at home. But when they did, they received support from no one. And more often than not, others in the community ignored the persons with disabilities as though they did not exist.
- Other families—after much anguish—did allow their children to be sent to institutions. However, they did it because training and treatment programs were promised. In many cases, such programs were really nonexistent, but what could the parents do? After all, agencies in the community promised nothing.
- Whenever a civilization is successful in total repulsion, one needs to keep a close eye on the patterns that follow. For example, such an act took place in Germany in 1940. Author Wilhelm Tuefel, in *Das Schloss Der Barmherzigkeit* (Stuttgart: Quell-Verlag, 1960), described how the Nazi Party accepted the doctrines of philosopher Karl Binding and physician Alfred Hoche, who declared that persons with substantial handicaps were entities whose lives were "devoid of value" and should be "released." They actually meant "killed," but in print, that word must have seemed too harsh. Then Tuefel described how two gray buses with painted windows picked up residents at an institution in Stetten and transferred them to a crematorium in a castle called Grafeneck, some miles away. It didn't take long for the word to spread throughout the countryside that the residents of the institution were being destroyed. And when the word reached the parents of those people with handicaps, according to Tuefel, they reacted in one of three ways: Some hurried to the institution and took their relatives home; others came to say goodbye (some terrible farewell scenes were described); and some did not come at all.

But the story of that country's repulsion of persons with disabilities did not stop there. There is evidence showing that the technology and management skills finally used in the German death camps were first perfected in institutions for people with handicaps.

Today it is interesting to note that we no longer worship the idea that our civilization is continuously progressing toward perfection. Such a belief first fell apart when our minds tried to comprehend Buchenwald, Auschwitz, Hiroshima, and Nagasaki. At this point in history, we do not know whether the world is getting better and better—we only know it has gotten more complex. And yet, it is an astonishing fact that the general public's healthy interest in persons with developmental disabilities began to mushroom after the Holocaust and the Atom Bomb. One cannot help wondering if there is a connection.

7

No Overwhelming Army Here

During the twentieth century, the number of people *thought* to have developmental disabilities has declined radically.

• In 1913, when immigration into the continent was high, some of the leading psychologists and sociologists claimed it was a scientific fact that the world's morons, idiots, and imbeciles (the standard diagnostic labels of that period) would outbreed the "normal" people. At that time those scientists believed there were more people with subnormal intelligence than with normal and above and that if such feebleminded ones were not segregated and sterilized, and if others were not stopped from emigrating into the continent, North America would teeter and slide off into a terrible moral and intellectual decline.[1]

• During World War I (1918), those same scientists claimed that the world was already slipping into the degeneracy they had predicted. For example, an intelligence test, a modification of the Stanford-Binet, was administered to draftees in the United States Army, and it was claimed that better than half our fighting men were feebleminded.[2]

• By 1965, the number of persons with mental retardation was statistically estimated to be 3 percent of the population. However, there was a discrepancy between the estimated and the actual: It seemed that only 1 percent was locatable at any given time.[3] That was quite a drop from the 1920s.

• In 1977, the number of *all* persons with developmental disabilities was estimated by the United States government as being a tiny 1.4 percent of the population![4]

What happened?

• We have become more knowledgeable about who is and who is not developmentally disabled.

• The penchant to label as feebleminded anyone whom we fear or do not understand has decreased.

• The myths about persons with handicaps are quietly retreating as the real developmental problems are identified.

• More and more communities are no longer seeing these persons as an overwhelming army.

Neighborhoods will discover that there are not enough of these citizens with handicaps to go around. Some neighborhoods will have to do without!

---

1. Clarence Karier, "Testing for Order and Control in the Corporate Liberal State," in N. J. Block and Gerald Dworkin, eds., *The I.Q. Controversy* (New York: Random House, Pantheon Books, 1976).
2. R. M. Yerkes, *Psychological Examining in the United States Army,* vol. 15 (Washington, D.C.: Memoirs of National Academy of Sciences, 1921).
3. President's Committee on Mental Retardation, *Mental Retardation: The Known and the Unknown* (Washington, D.C.: DHEW Publication No. (OHD) 76-21008, 1976).
4. The National Task Force on the Definition of Developmental Diabilities (HEW's Developmental Disabilities Office) made the following estimates: mental retardation .5%, cerebral palsy .3%, epilepsy .25%, autism .05%, learning disability .1%, all other developmental disabilities .2%.

8
Becoming More Intelligent About Intelligence

An eighty-three-year-old woman in Omaha gave me an interesting explanation of mental retardation. When she was casually asked how she felt about her new neighbors, she said,

I get along very well with the fellows. We speak to each other as we pass on the sidewalk, and I think it's great the way those young workers train the men the way they do. . . . But isn't it sad? After all, you and I know *there wouldn't be any mental retardation in people if it wasn't for loose women.*

Today, it is possible to laugh at such a belief. But when that woman in Omaha was a teen-ager, nobody laughed. Many leading psychologists and sociologists of that day viewed as a scientific fact the theory that persons having "good blood" were virtuous and pure in heart, while the lineage of "bad blood" was laced with trollops—and that anybody with that heritage simply had to be feebleminded, too.

Here is how it came about. In the early 1900s, Alfred Binet developed a series of puzzles and stunts, which he tried out on two hundred schoolchildren in Paris, France, in an attempt to define intelligence. He died, however, before coming to any final conclusions. Then around 1910, Lewis Terman, a professor at Stanford University, tried Binet's puzzles on some children in California. American children didn't do well on French stunts, so Terman rewrote the series, using puzzles that middle-class California students could understand, and called it the Stanford-Binet Intelligence Test. Terman and a number of the nation's leading researchers coupled the Stanford-Binet with Mendel's data on the breeding of pea plants, and they began a push to develop a pure race of people. Their movement contained some powerful thrusts that strongly conditioned the thinking of people living at that time, such as the neighbor in Omaha.

• In 1912, a best-selling book entitled *The Kallikak Family* (New York: The Macmillan Co.) was written by Henry Goddard, the director of the research laboratory at the Training School for Feebleminded Girls and Boys in Vineland, New Jersey. Goddard, applying the Stanford-Benet test and the pea-plant data, told the story of Martin Kallikak, Sr., a noble Revolutionary soldier of "good English blood" who, at a tavern frequented by the militia during the war, met and slept with a "feebleminded woman." By this woman, he became the father of a feebleminded son. Although Martin, Sr., was far away at the time of the birth, the woman, in a not-so-feebleminded way, named her son Martin Kallikak, Jr. Goddard described how Martin, Sr., this "scion," this noble soldier, "in an unguarded moment, steps aside from the paths of rectitude and with the help of a feebleminded girl, starts a line of mental defectives that is truly appalling." Goddard claimed to have identified four hundred eighty descendants, of whom many were feebleminded, as well as illegitimate, sexually immoral, and alcoholic. There were prostitutes, epileptics, criminals, paupers, perverts, welfare clients, whorehouse madams, horse thieves, and one was even "of the Mongolian type." After a list like that, one has to admit that Goddard was capable of delivering one powerful sermon against sowing wild oats. But that was only half his study. He continued,

Martin Sr., on leaving the Revolutionary Army, straightened up and married a respectable girl of good family, and through that union has come another line of descendants of radically different character. These now number 496 in direct descent. All of them are normal people. . . .

All of the legitimate children of Martin Sr. married into the best families of their states, the descendants of colonial governors, signers of the Declaration of Independence, soldiers and even the founders of a great university. Indeed, in this family and its collateral branches, we find nothing but good representative citizenship. There are doctors, lawyers, judges, educators, traders, landholders; in short, respectable citizens, men and women prominent in their communities wherever they have gone.

After this book and a few others like it were published, the good blood/bad blood theory became extremely popular. It set off what came to be known as the "eugenic scare," which spread rapidly throughout the land.

• In 1912, Goddard was invited by the United States Public Health Service to test newly arriving immigrants at Ellis Island. By 1913, his report, "based on a mass of average immigrants," showed that 80 percent of the Hungarians, 79 percent of the Italians, and 87 percent of the Russians were feebleminded. He stated that the Polish, in the ninetieth percentile, were the most feebleminded of all the immigrants (which may explain the quality and prevalence of Polish jokes). On the other hand, immigrants from England, Holland, Denmark, Scotland, and Germany were found by Goddard to be the most intelligent.[1] According to this data, if you want to be a high-grade, bright individual, you shouldn't let yourself be born in any country east of Germany.

• During World War I, when Robert Yerkes of Harvard University conducted the mass testing program for two million draftees, he made his discovery that over half the United States troops were subnormal. According to his tests, the average soldier had a mental age of fourteen.[2] These results, however, were not published until 1921, so the country never knew until the war was over that better than half its troops were not fit for battle.

• Lothrop Stoddard, in *The Revolt Against Civilization* (New York: The Macmillan Co., 1922), carefully distilled all the intelligence scores from across the nation—including the army test scores—and he claimed, also, that the average mental age of Americans was below average. (His average boiled down to the fourteen-year-old mind, as well.) Walter Lippmann, writing in *The New Republic* in 1922, stated that Stoddard's conclusion "is precisely as silly as if he had written that the average mile was three-quarters of a mile long."

• Later, Yerkes and his colleagues admitted that the army tests were geared not only for discovering feeblemindedness, but also were carefully timed so that 4.5 percent would receive an A. That was the number of men from the masses that the army needed to send to officer's

training school. When Lippmann learned of this, he wondered what would have happened to the timing—and to the rest of the men taking the test—if the army had needed only half as many officers.

• *If we don't stop them, they will outbreed us*—this became the ultimate myth. It was felt that the good blood of the "meritocracy" must never become defiled by the bad blood of the feeble-minded masses. So in the 1920s we tested within the country for feeblemindedness, and we filled institutions with those the test rated in that category. At Ellis Island, we tested newly arrived immigrants, and those who were found to be "feebleminded" were denied entry into the country. This was easily done because, in 1924, Congress passed an immigration law assigning "national origin quotas," utilizing recommendations and reports prepared by Goddard, Terman, Yerkes, and their colleagues. Soon afterward, the Stanford-Binet was radically modified into a more abbreviated test. Alistair Cooke, in *America* (New York: Alfred A. Knopf, 1975), described how it was used at Ellis Island:

The newcomers crowded into the main building and the first thing they heard over the general bedlam were the clarion voices of inspectors bellowing out numbers in Italian, German, Polish, Hungarian, Russian and Yiddish. According to assigned numbers they were herded into groups of thirty and led through long tiled corridors up a wide staircase into the biggest hall most of them had ever seen. . . . Once they were assembled there in their thousands, the clearance procedure began. . . .

They moved in single file through a stockyard maze of passageways and under the eye of a doctor in a blue uniform who had in his hand a piece of chalk. He was a tough instant diagnostician. He would look at the hands, the hair, the faces and rap out a few questions. He might spot a panting old man with purple lips, and he would chalk on his back a capital "H" for suspected heart disease. Any facial blotches, a hint of gross eczema brought forth a chalked "F" for facial rash. Children in arms were made to stand down to see if they rated an "L" for the limp of rickets or some other

---

1. Leon J. Kamin, "Heredity, Intelligence, Politics and Psychology: II," in *The I.Q. Controversy*.
2. *Psychological Examining in the United States Army*, vol. 15.

deficiency disease. *There was only one chalk mark that every family dreaded, for it guaranteed certain deportation. It was a circle with a cross in the middle, and it indicated "feebleminded."*

Civilization has come a long way since then. The testing and culling craze of the early 1900s has given way to intelligence researchers who have begun to focus on every aspect of hereditary and environmental influence. And not one of them has come up with easy, dualistic, good-guy-versus-bad-guy theories. On the contrary, they see a richness, a complexity, and a deepness in each person that earlier testers never even dreamed existed. For example, *Psychology Today,* in September, 1979, developed a special issue on intelligence testing. A new breed of researchers described the present situation, and almost all the writers honestly admitted that, with what is now known about the human mind, *they do not know what intelligence is.* And if one can't define it, how can one test for it?

Make no mistake—those researchers did not make such statements because of a lack of knowledge, but from an additional appreciation of the great complexity and potential of each human mind. The editor of the magazine summarized it this way.

Now, the brave new world of intelligence research is beginning to come up with some answers. At universities and research centers across the country psychologists are coming to believe that *intelligence may not be just one thing:* it may be many different things—some of them ignored by IQ tests. Ironically, intelligence in real life may truly be a multiple-choice proposition.

This knowledge is good news for you and me—and for our neighbors with handicaps. It means that our society no longer needs to view people as if they were so many pebbles on a beach that need to be labeled "above average" or "below average" and classified along a single, monotonous line. The penchant for testing and culling people is over.

9
The Good Life Is Relative

Great philosophers are not the only ones who have sought the good life. They have created schemes for "the pursuit of true happiness," "the highest good for the greatest number," and the combining of "truth, beauty, and goodness," but we, too, have visions in our minds of the ideal life, whether we are mothers, machinists, maids, mail-carriers, martyrs . . . or anyone else.

Also, we know that some brilliant members of our communities may not necessarily find life as good as do some of us who have less intellectual functioning. For example, Nicholas Noodle was one who had moved through the University of Nebraska with remarkable ease; he graduated summa cum laude, and several prestigious organizations offered him jobs. On the other hand, Sam Messina, at the same age, came home to tell his parents that he had graduated from the industrial training center for persons with developmental disabilities and had been accepted as a member of the dishwashing-work-station crew at the Omaha Methodist Hospital. His starting pay was the minimum wage. But that was not all: His counselor had notified him that there was an opening for him at an adult-supervised apartment, where he would live with two other men with handicaps and a live-in residential trainer. The joy at the Messina home was so great that night that the neighbors and some of the people who worked with Sam were invited to a special celebration at Caniglia's Restaurant on the following Saturday.

In the past, civilization automatically would have rated Noodle's accomplishments highly, while Messina's would have been seen as insignificant. Nevertheless, if some new metering device could be plugged into both these men to measure the ergs of energy each had expended in improving himself during the last five years, an interesting fact might be discovered: Messina's *effort* probably would have been greater than Noodle's. And Messina probably would be experiencing a greater sense of accomplishment, as well.

Of course, we already knew that energy expended in a self-improvement task can influence an individual's sense of satisfaction in life. Now, however, people with handicaps are dramatizing this fact as never before.

• Elmer Cogburn left a midwestern institution at age nineteen to work as a farmhand in northern Kansas. He became the subject of a beautiful arrangement, in which three different farmers set him up in an apartment in a small town and scheduled him for a rotating but full-time job. When he was twenty-one, I paid him a visit and over supper, he told me about his work. He was proud of his strength. "It was hard at first, but now I can load bales as fast as any of 'em." He explained how he placed his spending money in seven piles in his top dresser drawer—one pile for each day of the week. Then he produced his bankbook, showing $200 in the asset column. Throughout the meal he talked about his "spreads"—the three farms. As the visit ended, it was obvious that *Elmer Cogburn experienced the same sense of accomplishment that you or I would, if we had owned the three farms.*

• Donald Shannon, a nine-year-old boy with atrophied legs, was learning to move his wheelchair up a fifty-foot ramplike hall in a special-education program in Topeka, Kansas. He was promised a job as a mail messenger if he made it. On the back of the wheelchair was a sign: DON'T PUSH ME. I GOTTA DO IT MYSELF. The young man accosted that rising hallway five days a week, for more than two months, in unsuccessful attempts to reach the top. During that period, frustration, tears, and anger were daily companions. Then he made it, and nearly thirty people gathered around him and applauded. He had never before received such cheers from so many people in his whole life. That day it was obvious that *Don Shannon was experiencing the same thrill that you or I might enjoy if we had reached the summit of Mount Everest.*

• Jimmy Kelly is a nine-year-old boy with multiple handicaps: blindness, mental retardation, cerebral palsy, and occasional epileptic seizures. His father is a graduate of the U.S. Naval Academy and is now a corporation executive in Pittsburgh; and his mother is an outstanding educator. Both parents are members of Mensa, an organization for people with the highest intelligence in the nation. Jimmy's brothers and sisters—all teen-agers—are definitely following in their parents' footsteps when it comes to learning. In the past, the presence of a child with handicaps in a family where learning is prized so highly would have been extremely threatening. Not so in this family. The tenderness observed at mealtimes—even with Dad taking charge at the late dinner; the different interactions with Jimmy that each of the siblings carries out; the training of neighbors as sitters and emergency helpers; the family camping trips that include Jimmy—all this and more helps one to see that Jimmy's tiny developmental milestones (such as overcoming a gagging reflex, moving to solid foods, and nonverbally communicating joy and affection for other family members) are valued as highly as the major accomplishments of others in the family. Although Jimmy has never experienced anything but this calm, purposeful, and nurturing environment, he *knows he is valued*. And this family experiences richer interactions and zest for living because Jimmy is there.

Today, as never before, you have an opportunity to know such people in your own neighborhood and to sense how hard they have worked to get where they are in their developmental climb. Of course, you will find some who are bitter with life, just as many so-called normal persons have developed sour views. Nevertheless, you are in a position to develop a respect for a certain farmhand, dishwasher, motel maid, or pieceworker; or a person who has just learned to eat his or her own meals; or another who, with imperfect speech, has learned to say hello to you and call you by name.

Citizens with handicaps may help you to learn about another definition of the good life. For neighbors with handicaps, the good life is

    solving one's own problems

    at one's own level

    with one's own abilities.

Successes like these may prove to be more satisfying and richer than those in your life or mine.

Courage and Heroism—
They Have Them, Too

On July 2, 1972, six young men drowned in the Missouri River while trying to save one another. Five were residents of a small-group home in Omaha, operated by the Eastern Nebraska Community Office of Retardation. The sixth was a dedicated, well-liked staff member.

On this long Fourth of July weekend, they and a few others had been fulfilling a long-sought wish to "rough it" at Indian Cave, Nebraska's newest, most primitive state park. These citizens with handicaps—many of them former residents of institutions—and some staff members had become avid campers. And all were experiencing a rich new high in their personal development—until the group began to wade in a large, placid-looking inlet of the Missouri River, which bordered the camping area.

Then it happened! One man moved past an underwater ledge; he became caught in an undertow and was dragged down. Others went to his aid, only to find themselves caught in the river's overpowering force as well. Some were pulled to safety, but when they saw others in trouble, they went back in again to help. Within five minutes six men were lost, while the rest moved ashore, dazed and exhausted.

Six times during the next ten days, a body was found downstream; and six times a church or a mortuary was packed, inside and out, with Omahans from all walks of life. There were friends (many with handicaps, who had known one another at institutions), relatives, neighbors, professionals, government officials, and volunteer workers—all drawn together by a common grief.

In the aftermath, many honored the staff member posthumously: The county board made a special award; a national convention of the Student Council for Exceptional Children was renamed as a memorial; statements about this man's courage were published, and all were deserved. There is no doubt—he could have saved himself, but he did not.

However, after visiting the site of the tragedy, talking to staff members, attending six funerals, and listening to the other citizens with handi-caps who were involved in the incident, a haunting question stuck in my mind: *Why did fewer people recognize heroism in the five other men?*

I attempted to solve this problem by referring to a concept called *the dignity of risk,* which concluded that people with handicaps were often overprotected; that others made choices for them that they could have made for themselves; and that they often were kept from experiencing and growing from failure. The concept points out that healthy development can be increased by risk-taking and that its absence can be crippling. This principle answered part of the question that had grown out of the incident at Indian Cave. But part remained unexplained.

Five years later, the rest of the riddle was solved for me. On April 9, 1977, I watched Dr. Leonard Kriegel *walk* on his crutches—his polio-smitten legs trailing—up to the podium of the McGraw-Hill Conference Center in New York. This gutsy, defiant man, a professor of English and the author of *The Long Walk Home,* spoke to authors and scriptwriters who had gathered to take a closer look at the way people with handicaps were being portrayed in the media. Kriegel spoke movingly about *the cripple as hero.* Armed with many key quotations from English literature, he built his case point by point. "It is not so much the failure of courage in the cripple. It is that others *prevent* them from being courageous."

Then it became clear to me that society, in the past—because of its own sense of uncertainty, weakness, and distorted needs—was often unable to recognize citizens with handicaps as heroes.

After all, if I act strong and heroic, when inwardly I do not *feel* heroic, something within me may forbid that I recognize one of *them* as a hero. However, the more I feel OK about people with handicaps *and about myself,* the less time I need to waste on such bluffs.

Today, you and I have renewed opportunities to search among the cowards of the world for heroes. After all, heroes are really cowards who "hung in there" longer than the rest of us. And this time, with our new views, heroes with handicaps will be right up there on the list with people who are not handicapped. My list now contains

a man with Down's Syndrome, who died trying to rescue his brother from a burning house;

a woman with cerebral palsy, who pulled an angry, biting, police dog off a seven-year-old child;

a teen-ager with retardation, who calmly cared for his friend who had been floored by a seizure in a theater lobby, and through his explanations to bystanders, helped them to relax and even to be touched by his ability to care for his friend;

a woman with Down's Syndrome, who stayed all night at the bedside of a seriously ill, elderly neighbor who lived in the next apartment.

There are more on my list who are heroes because of specific acts of loyalty, kindness, perseverance, and sacrifice. It is my hunch that you can look quietly around your neighborhood and add some heroes like these to your list, as well.

11
Love, Tenderness and Marriage:
Some New Sensitivities and Supports

Attitudes toward citizens with developmental problems are changing so rapidly that some of the things that are happening now could not have been predicted even ten years ago. For example, in the spring of 1979, the Columbia Broadcasting Company presented a two-hour television special, "No Other Love," a touching story of a man and a woman with mental retardation—who fell in love and were married. One month later, the American Broadcasting Company also aired a feature about the marriage of persons with retardation. ABC's presentation, "Like Normal People," was based on the book of the same title (New York: McGraw-Hill, 1978) by *Washington Post* reporter Robert Meyers, who wrote about his brother Roger and Virginia Hensler, who were helped to develop an emotional partnership, in spite of their handicaps. Both of these television specials received high audience ratings and national awards; Meyers' book has been widely read, and it, also, has received national honors.

There is cause for amazement here: An issue that once was squelched and swept under the rug is now being broadcast to all North Americans. A few years ago, men and women with handicaps had been forced to exist apart from one another. Most institutions were built so that dormitories for males and females were situated on opposite sides of large grassy expanses. Men and women were together in some places such as dining halls, but even there they did not sit together, and they were never beyond the watchful eyes of their caretakers. All longings for close friendships with the opposite sex were blocked. As if being deeply wounded by disabilities were not enough for these people, this additional injury was inflicted upon them.

Society, for unclear reasons, believed that all people with developmental disabilities possessed horrid antisocial traits that could be passed on to their offspring and that if their sexuality were not dammed up, a raging river of fornication would ensue, leading to the degeneration of humankind. Such generalizations were brutally unfair; nevertheless, civilization continued to impose rigid rules, especially in institutions, attempting to snuff out all sexual development in these defenseless people. One midwestern institution even went so far as to castrate males who masturbated; many states and provinces mandated that females be sterilized before they were discharged from institutions. Fortunately, such blind oppression is receding rapidly in both the United States and Canada, and it is my belief that neither will ever permit citizens with handicaps to suffer such extreme cruelties again.

When Roger Meyers and Virginia Hensler fell in love, there was no attempt, as there would have been in the past, to brutally block their attraction for each other. On the contrary, an amazing number of people became involved in helping them examine and build on their love. Although the process was rocky (any courtship worth its salt is), an impressive number of assists from others are described in Robert Meyers' book.

• *The couple's right to love* was recognized and defended by key persons, although at first it was agonizingly difficult to convince some of the people in authority.

• *Training in community living* would have been provided regardless of their feelings for each other, but their marital plans were the couple's motivation, and learning became a serious undertaking for them. Success in cooking, housekeeping, grooming, working, receiving salaries, shopping, budgeting, choosing apparel, behaving appropriately, and riding public transportation became more important than ever before. And fortunately, a rich array of community-based services was available to help them accomplish these skills.

• *Genetic testing* was performed on both Roger and Virginia, and no hereditary problems were found. They, like many other couples with handicaps, submitted willingly to such tests. Consequently, such people usually know more about the condition of their genes than does the average person.

• *Emotional relationships* were discussed in order for them to develop an understanding and a tenderness for each other. Each learned when something could cause pain to the other and how to control such disturbing activities.

• *Sex education* was thorough. "Roger and Virginia knew about sex, about intercourse, about orgasms, about pregnancy, and about everything else that people in their twenties know about," wrote Robert Meyers.

• *Whether or not to have children* was a problem that Roger and Virginia struggled with for some time. Roger wanted children, but as their counselor, Bill Stein, gradually helped them to experience more and more of their brave new world of independence—and the heavy responsibilities that came with it—they decided against parenthood. Although the book does not say so, one can surmise that even a responsible decision in favor of having children would have been supported.

• *The breaking of parental controls* is seldom easy. Even with so-called normal couples, such proclamations of emancipation can cause stormy times. Consequently, people with handicaps— because of the additional parental protection that has been exerted for many years—will usually find it extremely difficult. After realizing that such couples must break away from parents and cleave to each other, the decision of the parents of Roger and Virginia to finally let go was not easy, but they made it.

• *Pastoral counseling* of a high quality was reflected in the marriage service. The pastor met with the couple repeatedly until all preparations for the wedding were carefully made and understood by the couple. When the service finally took place, Roger was so relaxed that he unexpectedly cued the pastor *sotto voce* about certain things he wanted said to the congregation.

• *Follow-up counseling* with the couple still takes place for several hours each week in their apartment. Robert Meyers described counselor Carol Knieff as

one of hundreds of young people around the country who work in the human-services field, helping to improve life for the retarded. Her job did not exist a

dozen years ago. Quietly and with infinite patience, she listens to Roger and Virginia talk and struggles with them as they attempt to express their thoughts. Carol makes suggestions on everything from menu planning to appropriate clothing for different occasions, and in subtle ways, she helps them steer themselves to a more normal life.

Twenty years ago, it would have been unthinkable that so many relatives, friends, professionals, neighbors, and volunteers would have pitched in and helped two citizens with handicaps responsibly plan their marriage. Nor would the rallying people have possessed the finely tuned knowledge and skills needed to support the marriage after the vows were made.

Now marriages between such persons are taking place throughout Canada and the United States, and it is my hunch that the success rate of these unions is higher than the national average. And as the rest of us become aware of the sophisticated, community-based training and support services that are becoming increasingly available, we may quietly wish we had such coordinated help for our own marriages.

But are some persons too handicapped for such emotional partnerships? Of course. And some may be working so hard to overcome specific barriers in their lives that they simply do not have time or interest in the opposite sex. Others may only want friends. And the beauty that can be found in the exploring of distances and closenesses between persons with handicaps lies in the fact that *more and more, they are being skillfully helped to make their own responsible decisions about their relations with the opposite sex.*

Marriage can be a madhouse. Or it can be the most energizing, life-stabilizing partnership two human beings can experience. And I think that unions such as the one of Roger and Virginia Meyers rate high on the latter list. For example, on December 9, 1977, while returning home from work at 11:45 P.M., Roger heard a cry for help from his neighbor, seventy-six-year-old Beatrice Houghtellin. He entered her apartment to find that she had fallen and smashed her head against the kitchen stove, breaking her nose and burning her face. Meyers calmly called the police and stayed with her until help arrived. Later he was honored for what he had done, and he received a $5 reward from Mrs. Houghtellin. This emergency gave Robert Meyers a chance to reflect on how far his brother and sister-in-law had come in their relationship.

The growth and maturity of Roger and Virginia Meyers since their June 18, 1977, wedding has been phenomenal. Their calmness, seriousness, and sense of self are just as stunning. The incident involving Mrs. Houghtellin is remarkable, precisely because it is such an unremarkable event: A neighbor needed help, and a young man called the police. It is the kind of responsible act that people do every day, but of which the retarded are thought incapable. Maybe they are, when they are given no real-life experience and when the expectations of their abilities are kept so low. So, maybe, it is time to revise upward our expectations of retarded persons.

12
New Zest in the Neighborhood

In one segment of interviews, I contacted 158 people living close to eighty-seven well-run familylike residences for citizens with handicaps. Then, using my own criteria, I rated each conversation:

29 percent were—to a large or small degree—warmly involved with their neighbors who were handicapped;

62 percent were neutral ("It makes no difference to me. Them or somebody else. I'm not all that involved with my neighbors," said one man who represented the general feelings of this group);

9 percent seemed a bit distant and fearful. None were openly hostile; however, it was obvious that I had received their names from the residences for persons with handicaps, so no one told me that such people should not be living there.

When the interviews were completed, I was struck by three realizations. First, I shuddered to think what these interviewees would have said about their neighbors twenty years earlier. Next, it appeared to me that the persons with handicaps living in these residences had better than average relations with their neighbors. Finally—although I already had rich glimpses of this realization—it was driven home to me that the presence of many of these persons with developmental disabilities had brought a new zest and a rejuvenation to their neighborhoods. Here are some glimpses.

Philadelphia, Pennsylvania. The East Mount Airy Neighborhood Association, Inc. (EMAN), affiliated with National Neighbors, a nationwide association of multiracial neighborhood organizations, has learned that handicapped residents definitely can enrich the community. This middle-class neighborhood organization in a twenty-by-eighteen-block area in northwest Philadelphia, began in 1966 to "Make a Good Community Better" (their motto). In the midst of a beehive of campaigns—fighting urban blight, doing away with graffitti, establishing fair zoning, organizing block security routines, and developing youth programs, as well as initiating countless other efforts to beautify and humanize their neighborhood—they still had the energy and alertness to answer a newspaper advertisement seeking homes for residents who were moving out of Pennhurst, a nearby institution for persons with handicaps. EMAN's six officers and thirty-six-member board studied the situation, and in 1971, they agreed to develop four residences—ordinary houses on ordinary streets—at scattered locations in the community. When the citizens with handicaps moved into those homes, they immediately began substantial development, and the neighbors became invigorated as they watched them grow. As a result, EMAN has now added four semi-independent apartment units for persons who have developed beyond a need for the more intimate structure of the group homes. Now the neighborhood is planning for the day when the people in the apartments will be ready to move out on their own. Today, there is no doubt in the minds of the members of EMAN that their neighborhood is better because people with handicaps live there.

Jamestown, California. The mountain-loving people of Tuolumne County (population 22,169) are determined to take care of their own. Mark Twain and Bret Harte lived with and wrote about the colorful individualism of these Californians during the gold-rush days, and there is no doubt that the same spirit remains today. One citizen in Jamestown (population 950) put it this way.

We who live in these mountains are different. We like the way we are and we don't intend to change. But something aches inside when our handicapped children must move to the cities in the valley for special programs. They get help all right, but something is lost in the process. . . . Sometimes they no longer appreciate good mountain living like the rest of us do.

These people know that formal education has power, but they also have the good sense to know that there is another form of education that is just as important. Anthropologists call it *encul-*

turation. In this community, enculturation has to do with feeling in harmony with trees, gulches, rivers, and peaks; learning how to sense, nod, wink, speak, and generally interact with the rest of this close-knit community, and to do it so well that no one would ever mistake a Jamestown resident for one of the many tourists who flow through the town.

As a result, four semi-independent apartment residences for persons with developmental disabilities have been set up in a recently constructed forty-four-unit apartment complex, and nine teen-agers and adults who needed to move out of their family homes now live there. No licensing is required because the residents pay their own rent and the salary of the live-in supervisor from the supplementary support they receive from the government. The rest of the support services are handled by volunteers.

But the most striking aspect of the program has to do with the way these persons blend into the community. It may have started when the residents with handicaps, helped by the volunteers, began having potluck suppers and inviting local citizens to be their guests for dinner. Consequently, many of the persons with handicaps were invited to other homes for dinner. Spontaneous activities are going on continually: auto trips, fishing trips, movie and restaurant outings, churchgoing. The on-the-street relationships are rich, too. One only needs to walk through the town with one of the residents with handicaps, to hear the many Hello-theres, It's-good-to-see-yous and What-have-you-been-up-tos that these persons receive. One can sense the low-key but warm attitude of caring and responsibility that the townspeople have assumed. And yet in no case did anyone seem overprotective.

Since my interviews, I have been notified that the people of Tuolumne County have become aware of six other persons from the county who have severe and profound handicaps and who have been living in institutions for years. Nevertheless, the county feels that those people belong to this mountain culture, too, and it has begun to discuss the development of adequate community-based services for them, as well.

Greenwich, Connecticut. Many neighbors living in this suburb near New York City have reflected the same interest and pride in a small-group home for women with developmental disabilities that we found in the mountains of California. For example, there have been regular block parties in the neighborhood ever since the Greenwich Association for Retarded Citizens set up the group home in their midst. In many newspaper articles, neighbors have repeatedly stated their warm feelings for the women and the staff who live in the residence. One evening after having dinner at the home and visiting with some neighbors, I left with the feeling that a quiet catalyzing kindness radiates from the home and tends to draw the neighborhood a little closer together. Obviously there were many things that made it happen, and while I was there, I did discover one: Little children on the block know that any time they walk into the kitchen of the group home, there are cookies and milk waiting for them.

Spring Mount, Pennsylvania. When a middle-aged woman moved from an institution into an apartment in Montgomery County, outside Philadelphia, she was befriended almost immediately by the members of the local Mennonite church. Those gentle people were uncanny at sensing her struggle to adjust to a more independent life-style after so many years in a highly structured, regimented existence, and without being patronizing, they helped her become involved in an array of church and community activities. Then it was noticed that the woman's apartment was bleak. Although her job, packing electrical switches in a factory, paid more money than she had ever received before in her life, it still would take months to buy all the things she needed. So the Mennonite community held a surprise kitchen shower. And when she was forced to undergo surgery, the church provided some financial support until she returned to her job.

These gracious activities made it possible for the woman's case manager to step back and expend his energy elsewhere. In an interview, he said, "My working as a pro is fading. I'm just not needed on this case very much now. Those church people have created one of the best community support arrangements I have ever seen. And no matter how hard I worked, I couldn't even begin to duplicate what they have done for Margaret."

Tucson, Arizona. Wherever a small-group home is developed by Los Trepadores (The Climbers), one can observe an increased flow of friendly traffic between that residence and the neighboring homes. In one case, a TV camera crew from a local station arrived to film the activities of some children with severe and profound handicaps, but to do the filming, they had to set up their equipment in a neighboring house because the children were attending a birthday party there.

The group homes are scenes for many pleasant, neighborly coffee klatches. Staff persons with medical nursing backgrounds have placed themselves on call to the rest of the neighborhood. One neighbor child with severe asthma attacks and an elderly grandmother have been saved from crises by group-home staff who could come to their aid faster than anyone else.

Many of the neighbors who are near these privately developed homes know about specific barriers the residents are struggling to overcome, as well as the technologies that are being used to help them. Los Trepadores trains the staff persons to make it a point to explain such things to the neighbors every time there is a reasonable opportunity to do so. In the case of thirteen-year-old Sarah, who has severe behavior disorders, a next-door neighbor received such a clear explanation that she herself became involved in the therapeutic interventions. Sarah, who became attracted to the neighbor and her family, now enjoys "overnights" next door as a reinforcement for the healthy behavior she is developing. A staff member explained,

Little Sarah came to us as no cute kid. Her behavior was wild. That little girl could throw temper tantrums; she could empty our backyard of all the toys by throwing them over the fence into the neighbor's yard. Well, the neighbor family became interested in Sarah after we let them know how we planned to help Sarah get control of herself. Then we helped the neighbor to learn the reinforcement skills we were using with Sarah. And it just developed that Sarah could stay overnight with the neighbor family when things were going well. The plan has worked beautifully.

The neighbor said,

The staff helped me to learn how to reinforce good things Sarah is doing. It's worked so well, any idea of punishing the girl is out of the question. I'm amazed. You know, when my kids were growing up, I spanked them at different times. It makes me feel strange that *now* I've learned how to get better results without such punishments. . . . You know, we must do a lot of things from fear. Everybody's afraid of people they don't understand.

Rick Eck, the executive director of Los Trepadores, explained how the staff members and the persons with handicaps are encouraged to plan and carry out specific acts of graciousness each week with individual neighbors. They may give a freshly baked loaf of bread to the neighbor across the street or do yardwork for one who is ill—little things, done freely and with no strings attached.

There is now no doubt that some neighborhoods have been drawn closer together because residents with handicaps are present on their block or in their apartment complex. Also, evidence is accumulating to show that even communities that fought to keep such homes out had a change of heart after the people and their staff moved in. The love and respect that emanates from such homes as these have enriched many neighborhoods in both Canada and the United States.

13
Neighborhood Children Are Powerful Peer– Group Educators

Jay Novicki took the hand-off and proceeded to run around right end in a front-yard tackle-football game. Then he suddenly stopped in his tracks, looking dazed.

"Wait a minute," one of his would-be tacklers shouted. "Jay is having a seizure."

Jay continued to stand motionless with the ball in his arms for a few seconds. Then he became alert again.

"You OK, Jay?" his opponent asked. Jay nodded yes.

"OK. Get movin'. Here we come." And the game continued.

I observed this happening about four years ago in Omaha, when I was delivering some news articles to Jan Novicki, an editor, at her home. In between plays, I had hurried from the car to the front porch but held off ringing the doorbell to watch the editor's twelve-year-old, a lad with mental retardation and epilepsy, mix it up with a rugged gang of kids who were playing as earnestly as if Nebraska University were taking on Oklahoma.

In the early years of our country, persons with seizures were believed to be demon-possessed. And a response to Jay's seizure would have been remarkably different, had he been living in Salem, the Massachusetts Bay colony, in 1692. Then he might have been hanged. In later years his seizure could have earned him a one-way trip to an institution. But that was before we learned that the brain sends simple electrical currents—some on command and some not—to activate muscles throughout the body. And once in awhile, the brain can malfunction by sending the wrong amount of electricity, causing the body to be motionless (in minor cases) or to go into an intense convulsing action and even to fall (in major cases).

Even if Jay's seizure had been a major one, it is possible that his friends would have known how to keep him from having a nasty fall, to see that his tongue was not caught between clenched teeth, to turn his head to the side so his breathing channels were clear, and to help him rest or continue playing when he came back to con-sciousness as the errant electrical charges began to subside. Today seizures can be so understandable that neighborhood children can be trained to help a friend who is having one.

The incident involving Jay and his friends is an excellent example of peer-group education. The boys and girls on Jay's block are learning, in simple down-to-earth terms, what it means to have a handicap and how to relate to a person with a handicap. On the other hand, Jay is not sidelined from regular community experiences. Because of his friends, Jay is a robust lad who knows how to mix it up with the rest of the fellows.

Neighborhood public schools have begun to recognize the power of peer-group education, too. Dr. Lou Brown from the University of Wisconsin, which has close training relationships with the Madison Metropolitan School District, gave a touching rationale for such involvements at one of the symposiums on the United Nation's International Year of the Child (1979). He felt neighborhood school children should relate even to students with severe and profound handicapping conditions.

Children with severe and profound handicaps need to be in regular schools, too. The interaction between these handicapped students and other students is utterly remarkable. And why not? After all, the future parents of such handicapped children are in the schools, today. And what kind of attitudes, values and expectations will such parents need? Also, future doctors, teachers, lawyers, policemen and ministers are in the schools, too. They need to grow up with such children so they will understand them and not reject them. Therefore, we are making conscious and systematic attempts to make sure that every student has some kind of interaction with such handicapped people. And in some of the schools I work closely with, we train regular students to handle seizures in school . . . to work with handicapped students at recess, in the gym and the swimming pool . . . to hire out as baby sitters for handicapped children . . . to help some learn to ride the bus . . . to wheel students in wheelchairs to and from school. In many cases, regular students receive class credit for their involvements with handicapped persons. These students have become so attracted to one another, we can't keep them apart.[1]

---

1. Robert Perske, ed., *The Child with Retardation—The Adult of Tomorrow: An International Year of the Child Report Sponsored by the International League of Societies for the Mentally Handicapped and the Association for Retarded Citizens* (Arlington, Tex.: ARC—National Headquarters, 1980).

Today, wherever one finds outstanding special education going on in neighborhood public schools, one finds such educational pairings taking place, even in smaller towns. For example, in St. Pierre Collegiate High School, serving the towns of St. Pierre (population 916) and St. Malo (population 731) in the Canadian province of Manitoba, students are trained to be peer-group teachers of young people who have recently moved into group homes from an institution. And such training takes place on public transportation, in restaurants, and in grocery stores, as well as in all the other neighborhood facilities that one seldom becomes familiar with while living in an institution. The regional representative of the Canadian Association for the Mentally Retarded, Brian Law, who worked closely with a behavioral counselor from the Manitoba Department of Health and Social Development and with the school faculty in setting up the program, described what happened to the high school students: "These kids, in learning to care for their retarded friends, have developed an extremely strong sense of justice. I've seen them shed tears over certain things that happened to their retarded friends. *They have convinced me that the only public attitudinal change efforts that are worth anything are face-to-face programs.*"

As happenings like those in Omaha, Madison, St. Pierre, and St. Malo take place one feels that neighborhoods and their schools are fulfilling educational attitudes and accomplishments predicted by Harold Howe II, one of North America's leading educational experts, for the year A.D. 2024. He looks forward to the time when children will not be rewarded only for competing to get the most out of education for themselves. They will be rewarded also for their contributions to the achievements of others.

The student who is proficient at reading or mathematics or who does accurate and high-quality work in the sciences is not necessarily rewarded. The assumption is that he has done well because his particular combination of heredity and environment made the achievement possible. He deserves no recognition for measuring up to his potential. *What the schools increasingly reward is not the student's own achievement but his contribution to the achievement of others.* And the higher his own attainments in learning, the more he is expected to do in helping others to learn.[2]

Twenty years ago, who would have dreamed that the best education for living a full life would involve interaction between people who are handicapped and those who are not? And the best place for it to happen?—in ordinary neighborhood settings!

---

2. Harold Howe II, "Report to the President of the United States From the Chairman of the White House Conference on Education, August 1, 2024," *Saturday Review World,* August 24, 1974.

14
Natural Reinforcement—
Neighborhood Style

Science is wonderful, I feel sure. But it is sometimes a verification of things that some people already knew. For example, there always has been a neighborhood sage—a widow, a poet, a cop, a secretary, a truck driver, or a retired factory worker—who knew how to encourage growth. For some unclear reason, they became interested in you, and they quietly maintained a keen interest in the things you were doing. Then when you did something better than you ever had done it before, they bragged about you to everybody. They *recognized* you. Sometimes they even gave you mementos of appreciation—rewards you never expected. Because of those unforeseen kindnesses, legs have run faster, jobs have been done better, restitutions have been more cleansing to the soul, instances of I-give-up-it's-too-hard have been fewer, and poems have had richer messages for us all.

It was interactions such as these that experimental psychologists and educational researchers took into the laboratory and tried out on rats and chimpanzees. From those results, they developed modern training technologies, which human-service workers, as well as people in many other fields, are now using. Consequently, many current educational programs contain instructions having to do with, as one manual put it, the precise use of developmental climates where positive feedback contain (1) *tangible reinforcers* (food, money, and other material rewards), (2) *social reinforcers* (warm exclamations, kind words, hugs, pats, handshakes, etc.), (3) *optimal timing* (usually as close to the accomplishment as possible).

Now science can prove that such reinforcement procedures really work. Pigeons have been taught to play ping-pong; salesmen have doubled their sales records; and dolphins have been trained to leap out of the water like missiles headed for space. But most heartwarming of all, progress notes, data charts, and before-and-after video tapings show that society's earlier expectation of persons with handicaps was a gross underestimate. That fact is being proved every day in ordinary neighborhoods throughout the states and provinces of North America. Ordinary citizens are picking up on the finer points of making another feel simply great when a new plateau of achievement has been reached, and they are recrafting these procedures to conform to their own homespun styles.

Neighbors sense the need for reinforcement. It seems to come with *getting to know* people with developmental disabilities—or anybody else for that matter, because we all need reinforcement in one form or another if we are to survive. However, the need is more crucial for people with handicaps because in the past they received so little. In a taped interview, Richard Abruzzi, a truck driver living in a North Chicago apartment house, gave me a clear explanation of such a need as he talked about his friendship with Jack Callahan, who lived in the next apartment. Callahan was twenty-four and a former resident of an institution.

Did you see all those bowling trophies and all those certificates and award ribbons in his apartment? That guy has saved everything—every scrap of paper—where somebody thanked him or said something nice about him. He even has this bundle of cards and notes which he has kept for years. [The bundle has yellowed with age and it is held together by a thick rubber band.] Well, he can't read very well, but he knows what every one of them says. There's a picture postcard from Niagara Falls which an attendant on a vacation sent to him at the Dixon Institution back in 1968. He has a note from a psychologist from the institution who was moving away. The note thanked Jack for helping him load furniture on a truck. That's a most interesting bundle. It's the guy's history. When Margie [Richard's wife] and I are with Jack, he often brings out the bundle and we go over the notes with him. It's amazing. Everything that anybody ever did to recognize Jack is tied up in that bundle and those trophies and certificates.

And so Abruzzi described how Jack Callahan had saved almost every material reinforcement he ever received. Collecting such treasures is not unique, however. One can travel across the continent and find many other individuals with handicaps who cherish their own precious aging bundles of momentos.

Customers can be reinforcers. Al Filipponi, manager of The Donut Shop in downtown La

Mesa, California, knows this to be true. Although there are eight other bakers and salespeople working alongside twelve people with handicaps, he knows that the customers walking in the door also can be a valuable support to people with developmental disabilities. He explained.

Most customers don't know that they are the best trainers we have. For example, we had a retarded young lady who was extremely shy, so we gave her a tray of bakery samples and told her to go out and give them to the customers. She received so many kind responses from people that her shyness disappeared almost immediately. Giving samples to customers, pouring them an extra cup of coffee [in an area containing tables and chairs], and listening to their responses are excellent training devices.

Filipponi willingly invests heavily in free bakery samples and cups of coffee, quietly parlaying them into a rich system of reinforcement for his employees with handicaps. "Some of these people grew up without very many pats on the back," he said. "They are hungry for such things, and I set it up so they can get them." There must be some connection between these interactions and the fact that baked goods and coffee always seem to taste better at The Donut Shop.

Many different kinds of *neighbors are doing what comes naturally*. Wherever one travels, it is possible to find fresh applications of the reinforcement theory; all are tailor-made to fit specific situations and communities. Usually, these acts don't call attention to themselves and are not carried out rigidly, but blend so naturally into everyday relationships that it is hard to isolate them from other interactions.

• Bill Prolkowsky, manager of a business in Kansas City, in the course of an ongoing friendship with Robert Donohue, found that Bob always had a rough time adjusting to a new job. He explained what he had seen happening and what he did about it.

Bob's mental retardation wasn't really his biggest problem. It was because he was so fearful and unsure of himself in a new situation. For example, he would take a new job—then after a few days, he would start thinking his boss didn't like his work and might fire him. So Bob—fearing he's going to get the ax—starts calling in sick or coming to work late. And sure enough, he would be fired. Well, I made Bob promise me that when he took the job washing pots and pans at Johnson's Cafeteria, *he would stick it out one month*—no matter what he thought the boss was thinking. And I promised him the biggest steak I could buy him at the Golden Ox Restaurant on the last day of the month if he stuck it out. During the month, it was rough—there was panic! But, do you know, at the end of the month, Bob and I had those steaks! By then, his work at Johnson's was going reasonably well, too.

• Maggie Roggerio, in Los Angeles, is a widow with five grown children, who now has focused her attention on two men and four women who live next door in a group home for people with development disabilities. Maggie has not become a certified trainer, but what she does for her neighbors has led to some remarkable achievements. She likes to cook, and for her, judging from the way she prepares Italian pastas, sauces, meats, and wines, cooking is loving. She quietly watches the progress of her neighbors and asks many questions of the group-home staff about what each one is doing. When she learns of a new plateau reached, she does what comes naturally: She throws a dinner party! "The most recent supper," said one of the staff, "took place last week after Sara Browning, a woman with Down's Syndrome, had successfully completed a one-to-one travel-training course, riding the bus to Pasadena and back. [Now Sara travels there on her own, to her job as a maid in a hotel.] I don't know of another group home in the world that has a neighbor like Maggie." The staff member was probably right. And yet it is altogether possible that there are as many different reinforcement procedures as there are people who have become good neighbors to people with handicaps.

On-the-street reinforcements are a possibility, too. After observing neighbors who consciously develop supports, I find myself wanting to strike up casual conversations with strangers who have handicaps. In some situations, starting a conversation with a person just because he or she has a handicap would be singling out, patronizing, or demeaning. When that is the case, I don't. And yet there are other opportunities when a conversation is appropriate. For example, on a crowded Conrail headed for New York City recently, I sat beside a man with cerebral palsy. For forty minutes, an interesting conversation took place: We shared our common concerns about the energy crisis, the coming presidential election, the rush-hour crowds at Grand Central, and root-canal dentistry. Of course, his speech was slow and slurred as he worked to sound the words, but that was OK; there was no rush. *And not once did either of us focus on the man's handicap.* Nevertheless, I felt our conversation was reinforcing to both of us.

Each of us sensed that we were saying some powerful things, nonverbally.

It's good being on the train with you.
You and I both have the right to be on this train exactly as we are.
You are looking pretty strong from here.
Keep going.
Have a nice day.

And so *repulsion,* the old neighborhood response to people with handicaps, dies out a little more each time a citizen rises up to utilize a new activity, *reinforcement.* And every time it happens, people with disabilities are liberated a little more. They receive the potential, dignity, and value that should have been theirs from the beginning.

15
It's OK to Ask About Property Values

Ownership of a piece of land and the house that's on it is a cherished privilege, and any threat to that ownership should not be taken lightly. So when the government decides to buy up property in order to build a superhighway, it can be expected that every now and then a person will be found sitting on the front porch of a home with a shotgun on his or her lap, daring the highway surveyors to set foot on that land. If someone decided to build a college fraternity dormitory next door to you, it also could be cause for alarm. It is understandable, then, that when a home for persons with handicaps is being set up next door—before you know all that is involved—you feel you have a right to know the real facts regarding the value of your own property.

Because citizens are concerned about the value of their homes, some states and provinces have wisely commissioned impartial research organizations to do studies on what happens when a group home is placed in a neighborhood. One of these studies was performed by Dr. Julian Wolpert and his colleagues from Princeton University, at the request of the state of New York.[1]

Wolpert's organization focused on 42 communities where the sales of 754 homes took place next door or across the street from homes for persons with developmental disabilities. At the same time they studied the sales of 826 homes in 42 similar communities that had no group residences. The research involved numerous contacts with neighbors, as well as the intensive study of documents and records of property transactions. Some remarkably clear findings came from that study.

• *The presence of group homes had no impact on property values at all.* The value of homes increased (or decreased) similarly to houses in communities where no group homes existed.

• *The proximity of a house to a group home had no effect on the market value;* even homes immediately next door to group homes did not decline in value.

• *The establishment of a group home did not generate a higher degree of property turnover* than that found in communities without such homes.

At the same time, the researchers focused on the placement, appearance, and functioning of the group homes. More valuable data was produced.

• *There was no evidence of neighborhood "saturation."* Persons with handicaps were never overrepresented in any of the communities studied.

• *The group homes looked like the other houses in the neighborhood.* They were of the same type and structure.

• *The function of the home was inconspicuous.* The average passerby did not know it was a group home for persons with developmental disabilities.

• *The group homes had a better appearance than the average home.* The repair and maintenance was better; even the lawns, bushes, and trees were better cared for.

Hard, clean facts like these have helped neighbors throughout New York state to dismiss any fears they may have had about property devaluation when persons with handicaps move into their neighborhoods. And when densely populated states dare to study the impact of group homes in communities like Albany, Bronx, Brooklyn, Buffalo, Hempstead, Kingston, Troy, Syracuse, Valley Stream, and Yonkers, the findings cannot help but diminish the fears of neighbors living in Tucson, Vancouver, Edmonton, Cut Bank, and Pumpkin Center.

1. Julian Wolpert, *Group Homes for the Mentally Retarded: An Investigation of Neighborhood Property Impacts* (Albany: New York State Office of Mental Retardation and Developmental Disabilities, August 31, 1978).

16
Zoning Laws Become Fair for Everyone

In 1977, the American Bar Association's Commission on the Mentally Disabled found that local governments were far too diverse to come up with uniform policies that were fair to both sides of conflicts centering on proposed residences for persons with developmental problems. For example, they found that members of an Ohio State University law reforms project worked intensely on handbooks and training programs that would help municipalities in Ohio develop fair zoning regulations. Sadly, after much investment of time, money, and energy, only eleven of Ohio's 930 local governments came up with zoning regulations that were just to everyone.

It then became clear to the bar association that only state and provincial governments possessed the distance and the objectivity to help local communities solve such conflicts. So they developed a model zoning law and—with the help of voluntary associations—began to lobby for it in state capitols.

Today their hard work has begun to pay off. States and provinces are developing fair zoning laws that even improve on the ABA model. Here are some of the components that can be found in these recent zoning practices.

• *Small groups of persons with handicaps will be treated as families.* They may live in an ordinary house on an ordinary street that is zoned for single-family dwellings. Also, they may live in ordinary apartments that are zoned for multiple-family dwellings. They do not need to be blood-related in order to live in this manner.

• *The number of persons in such a "family" is limited.* Most states and provinces are now saying that six or fewer persons with handicaps may live together. However, one national organization recommends that most of these homes contain only two or three such persons. This means that you and your neighbors can be protected from having a large dormitory or mini-institution next door.

• *Distance is required between group homes.* This ruling protects you and your neighbors from living in a concentration of such homes. The distances vary: Minnesota calls for the length of a football field (300 feet) between homes, while Michigan mandates better than half a mile (3000 feet), in large urban centers.

• *Political footballing is eliminated.* A few self-serving politicians once used such issues to their own advantage. They determined which side had the most clout and positioned themselves in front of that faction as its righteously indignant standard bearer, drawing many extra votes. But once the state or provincial law becomes clear, any politician would be a fool to engage in such a practice.

• *Special covenants no longer exclude people with handicaps.* It is all right for property deeds to contain special restrictions calling for such things as two-car garages, hidden garbage cans, and ten trees per plot. But any statement in a deed that could block people with handicaps from occupying a dwelling is declared null and void.

• *Licensing standards guarantee dignified, quality residences.* New zoning laws are seeing to it that licensing standards protect the dignity, rights, and developmental needs of both the citizens with handicaps and their neighbors.

• *Neighbors can monitor residential programs.* There is a monumental difference between a well-run, familylike residence and a place where persons with handicaps are "dumped" and forced to live a less-than-human existence. Since this is always a danger, you and your neighbors are in an excellent position to *learn* the zoning laws and licensing standards, to *monitor* the residential program, and to *advocate* for the persons with handicaps who live there. For example, if you observe that there is anything improper about the abilities of the staff members, the adequacy of the training programs, or the treatment of the residents, you and your neighbors have the right to communicate what you have seen to any or all of the following persons or agencies:

the staff members themselves;
the agency responsible for the home;
voluntary associations that advocate for the rights and dignity of persons with handicaps;
the state or provincial licensing agencies;
responsible elected officials.

Sensitive, commonsense monitoring by you and your neighbors is exactly what is needed in order to keep such group homes operating in the best way for those who live there. In many places, voluntary associations and government agencies support such monitoring and advocacy. Some even provide formal training for those who want it. Some, however, are just getting started. Ask around. Find out if there are organizations that are interested in supporting you in such efforts.

17
A Reflection on
Increased Funding

In 1950, so little money was spent on persons with developmental disabilities that nobody bothered to keep an accurate count. In 1978, however, local, state, provincial, and federal governments in the United States and Canada spent better than twenty billion dollars on these people.

What caused this change? Usually, we are quick to point out that the movement has

powerful voluntary associations

outstanding research and training agencies

remarkable technical breakthroughs

better than average coordination between volunteers and professionals

efficient lobbying strategies.

There is no doubt about it—these efforts form an amazing pattern of forces and have inspired governments to spend more than ever before in the support and training of persons with handicaps.

But is there not another underlying pattern—one that has been moving as silently and as powerfully as a small acorn turning into an oak tree? For example, since 1950, society's view of persons with developmental disabilities has quietly changed from seeing such persons as nonpersons, who could be expected to exist only in large groups of so-called nonpersons, to seeing them as valued, individual human beings, with the same weaknesses and strengths as the rest of us.

In my estimation, there is a definite correlation between civilization's *views* of such people and the money it *invests* in their support and training. In short, we are spending more because we *value* them more.

I always thought that when these people moved into the neighborhood, they would be heavy on our hands—loitering around, doing nothing. Well, I was wrong. They go to work during the day, they have programs at night, and on the weekends, they go with people to movies, plays, picnics, and recreational outings. I swear, they go to more things in a year than I will go to in a lifetime.

So spoke Maggie Roggerio, the celebration-giving neighbor in Los Angeles. Today, wherever community-based services are in place and working well, other neighbors are beginning to make the same observations.

For example, a person with a developmental disability may have only one individualized program plan and one program coordinator. Nevertheless, numerous agencies and individuals will, more often than not, produce different pieces of the plan. A truly comprehensive program plan will provide full services in at least three interlocking spheres.

Day Programs. The person with a handicap will usually go somewhere during the day—to school, to a vocational training center, or to a job. Even those with severe and profound handicaps are expected to have at least five and a half hours of daily programming.

Residential Programs. Special training usually takes place in the residences. Many persons with handicaps need to work, step-by-step, on specific skills that will enable them to live more independently in ordinary homes and ordinary communities—skills the rest of us often take for granted. In an apartment-living program in Oxnard, California, all the residents come home from day activities, work from 5 P.M. to 9 P.M. on week nights, and from 9 A.M. to 3 P.M. on Saturdays, on 148 different tasks in ten categories: meal preparation, money management, housekeeping, shopping, appliances, interpersonal relationships, communication, transportation, personal care, and safety.

Recreation and Leisure-Time Activities. Community recreation agencies, service clubs, churches, synagogues, athletic organizations, and special interest groups have been developing programs for people with handicaps. Many integrate such persons with their regular members in leisure activities. Also, a new movement of citizen advocacy organizations is springing up across the country, which screens, trains, and carefully matches ordinary citizens to those with handicaps, on a one-to-one basis. Citizen advocacies of an expressive nature call for regularly scheduled times together. Even more recently, self-advocacy organizations, in which people with handicaps elect their own leaders and develop their own programs, are keeping such people busy during the hours when they are not working, training, or sleeping.

Twenty years ago, not one of these programs was available, and persons with developmental disabilities would indeed have been heavy on the hands of other community members. Now, if they have too much time on their hands, it means that somehow the encompassing community-based service system has broken down. In many areas, the other extreme is more likely: People with developmental disabilities will be overprogrammed and will approach exhaustion if their individual program plans are not cut back.

Even so, many go through life investing much more time and energy than we do to master certain tasks. My friend Mike DiSilva dramatizes this fact every time he stays overnight with me. This young man with cerebral palsy must work extremely hard to control the poorly coordinated muscles in the right side of his face, as well as in his right arm and leg. In the morning, Mike, I'm sure, expends twenty times more energy than I do in order to get out of bed, wash, get dressed, eat breakfast, and go to work.

On the other hand, Mike has some neat consolations. He always will be handsomely thin. He burns so much energy in controlling his limbs and in speaking, that he can eat all he wants. He gets away with it; there is not an ounce of fat on his body!

And yet Mike and many others experience life as if they were sucking a thick malted milk through a very thin straw. They work incredibly hard for everything they get!

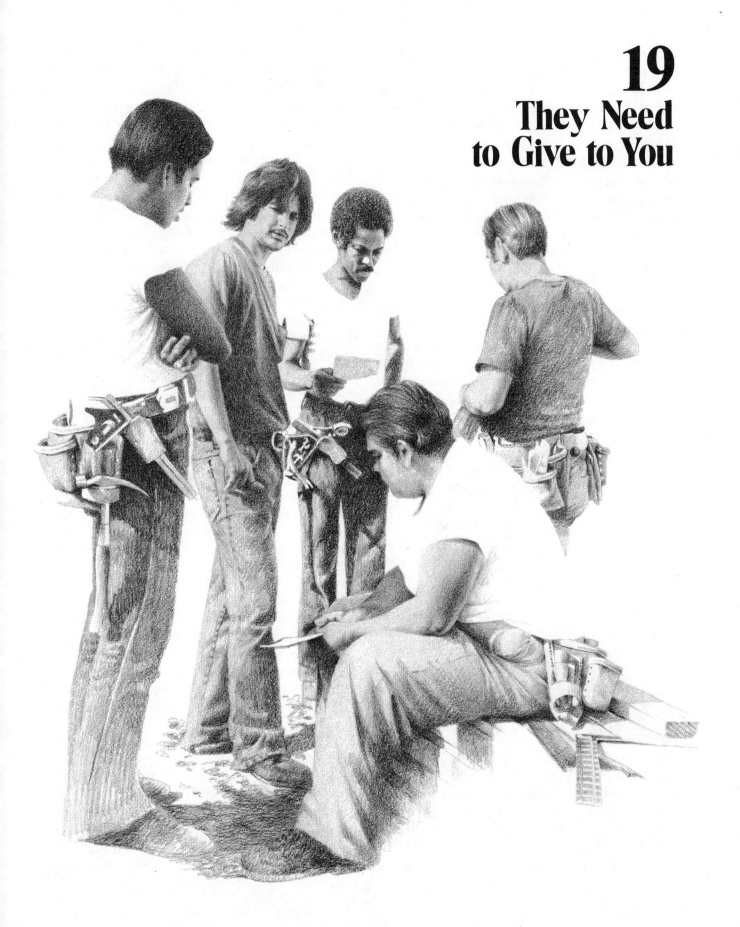

**19
They Need
to Give to You**

It is more blessed to give than to receive—as long as the giver does not have a handicap. Then it becomes embarrassing. After all, we should always be the ones who give (or so we thought).

Let me tell you about a downright humorous chain of events that took place at a state institution for persons with developmental disabilities, when thirty-two teen-age residents began pushing for a human right so obvious it is often overlooked—the right to give to others. The humor was present because aids and administrators alike had the good sense to see what the youngsters were fighting for and to make adjustments accordingly.

Ten days before Christmas in 1962, the corridors of the institution were filled with one community organization after another, singing Christmas carols. Although the singing was meant to bring cheer to the residents, it was obvious that many of the adolescents were bothered by it. Finally, in a group meeting, Harold, age seventeen, voiced displeasure of the visiting troubadors.

"It's not fair," he said. "All these people are singing to us when we can sing as good as they can. What the heck! There's gotta be some people we could sing to!" A few of us staff members, feeling sheepish because we hadn't thought of it, moved fast. Arrangements were made for the young people to go on caroling forays throughout the community, into ten different homes for the elderly. The project was an ineffable success.

However, this urge to give did not end with the holiday season. In January, the teen-agers raised an added concern: *Nobody would be singing to those old people until next Christmas. . . . That was a long time.* Consequently, with the help of staff members, the youngsters organized into three small service clubs and conducted Valentine's Day parties in the three homes having the greatest need for outside contacts. Then came special parties on St. Patrick's Day, April Fool's Day, and on it went, for more than two years.

Friendships began to develop between the institutional residents and the elderly residents,

through the many face-to-face encounters. That's when the real trouble began. The radio of an elderly man had been broken, and he sadly missed listening to the morning news. The three groups met together, in an attempt to figure out how they could buy their friend a new radio. Then it struck them: *Churches always take up offerings, but this was not done in their chapel services.* And so a request was sent to the administrators of the institution, requesting permission to put some of their coupons, which were used to buy candy and soft drinks, into an offering plate in their chapel services. They wanted the administrators to exchange the coupons for real money so they could buy their aged friend a radio. (Coupons were used because residents were not allowed to have real money in those days.) The administrators quickly denied the request. After all, top management thought, these poor unfortunate residents—who have so little in life already—simply could not be allowed to give away coupons from their dollar-a-week allowance. Nevertheless, the groups persisted, and the executives finally decided to give it a try. At that point one of the most democratic church-offering systems in the nation was born. Each Sunday the residents gave coupons, which were then deposited by the institution's accountant in a new category of the Patients' Benefit Fund. When a certain amount of money accrued, the residents *voted* on what they wanted to do with it. Then the accountant made out a check, which the residents used to carry out the designated mission. The first, of course, had to do with buying a radio.

In the fall, the residents voted to donate $325.28 *to buy food for hungry people overseas.* Again, the accountant prepared a check, payable this time to the Christian Rural Overseas Program, and the residents—with pomp and ceremony—delivered it to the local director of the relief agency.

Then came the time for the annual audit of the institution's financial records . . . and it does not take much imagination to visualize what happened when the state auditors found that state government checks had been written in order to

buy an old man a radio and to feed hungry people overseas!

When the investigation was over, and the smoke cleared, one of the auditors—after an if-you-quote-me-I'll-deny-it statement—quietly suggested that such expenditures be made in cash and that the notation in the accountant's books be less specific. Consequently, three more presentation rituals took place in the overseas relief agency's office, and more money was given to buy food for less fortunate people in other lands. However, at the climactic moment in each of these ceremonies there was no handing over of a government check. Instead, an outstretched hand offered a brown paper bag full of real money!

The giving continued. It ranged from special gifts for residents who were acutely ill ("When other people go to the hospital, they get gifts from their friends.") to twelve apple, peach, and pear trees, purchased and planted in a grassy area outside the institution's chapel. The tree project was undertaken because one member of the group stated, "Every kid should know what it feels like to steal an apple and run . . . and the little kids here have never had that chance."

The actions of these teen-agers forced all of us at the institution to face a haunting fact: The state had volume after volume of regulations describing how to give to the residents of this institution, but not one policy could be found that allowed the residents to give to others.

We have come a long way since 1962. People with handicaps are now organizing in order to become givers to the world, too. For example, the Center in Mental Retardation at California State University in Los Angeles has been putting together community redevelopment crews consisting of six people: a construction worker as crew chief and five men whose developmental disabilities render them incapable of being competitively employed. Then these men—with tool belts, hard hats, their own tool kits, and a together-we-can-do-things-none-of-us-could-do-alone philosophy—begin to perform amazing feats of service to others. Today, these crews are moving throughout Los Angeles County, constructing concrete ramps for wheelchairs and repairing and painting public and private rehabilitation facilities and homes for the elderly. These projects are completed for only the cost of the materials used. The crew chief receives a salary from a project grant, while the other men receive their usual government supplementary support checks.

From such labors, these men receive two important self-realizations: First, *they know that what they are giving is valuable to others.* Second, *they now feel that they are helping make the world a better place to live.* David Bilovsky, one of the creators of the program, believes such realizations are as important to these men as they are to us. He put it this way.

Right now, the federal government is trying to develop a welfare reform program that will separate those who can work from those who cannot. And would you believe that our handicapped workers are seen by the government as being among those who cannot work? What a shame! These men *are* working now. They *know* they have something rich to contribute to society. They feel it so strongly that they often come to work sick, and we have to send them home. It would be sad if these men are ever seen as nonproductive citizens and are sent home to live off the dole and watch TV all day.

Just last week, I was in a subway station on the East Coast, and it was in horrible disrepair. It made me want to bring our work crews to the city to begin working on those stations, one by one. Wherever I go, I see hundreds of public works projects that need to be carried out.

If Bilovsky is right, many persons with handicaps who are incapable of competitive employment could be tremendous forces in public works projects and community redevelopment, if we organize them effectively and value them for the contributions they can make.

But all the services I have described are *organized* acts. What about *individualized giving*? How can people with handicaps be helped to give on their own initiative—out of the goodness of their hearts?

I believe that you, the neighbors, are in the best position to be the receivers of such benevolences. And as it starts to happen, many people with handicaps will find another plateau of growth within reaching distance. Here's why.

• There are no family ties that bind you to your neighbors with handicaps, so they would feel no blood-related obligation to you.
• You have no professional relationship with such people, so your salary would not be dependent upon their behavior or upon your skill in eliciting it.
• You are not a trained volunteer worker, so there is slim chance that their giving to you would be of any great interest to your like-minded peers.
• You have the least amount of vested interest in these persons. So if they choose to give of themselves to you, it more than likely would be one of the most unselfish, unsolicited acts they could perform.

If you are aware of these facts, it may be easier to cast aside old feelings of embarrassment and to decide freely whether to accept the gifts they bring. And as I traveled, I found that individualized giving is on the increase.

• Two young women with developmental disabilities who live in a semi-independent apartment unit in Jamestown, California, have experienced a satisfying joy in cooking meals and inviting ordinary citizens from this small mountain town to be their guests. And while on a tour from Seattle to San Diego, I visited, observed, and interviewed, at forty-five different community residences and received twenty-one invitations from people with handicaps to be their guest for dinner. Of course, many did involve merely the cooking of TV dinners and the opening of cans. (However, nine times out of ten, that's all you would get if you received a last-minute invitation to my house.) What touched me most was the gracious way they invited me—wanted me to be with them—and the way they made me feel relaxed and at home.

• Benny Savidis, with a thirty-two-year history of institutionalization, was helped by John Zetsche, a staff member, to grow tomatoes in the backyard of their Chicago group home. Savidis, after three years' experience, now expertly tills a twelve-by-twelve-foot plot of ground each spring. Then he sets out thirty-six tomato plants ("Beefsteak tomatoes are my favorite."); he fertilizes, puts in six-foot stakes, ties up the vines, and regularly plucks the sucker sprouts ("You see, there should be only one limb coming out of the main vine at each joint—the rest are suckers and they have to be taken off."). Savidis' plants grow to the tops of the stakes, and it appears that his vines bear many more large, healthy tomatoes than the average. He obviously grows more of the red vegetables than are needed at the group home. So what does he do with the extra ones?

[Zetsche explained] Once a week, when they're coming ripe, Benny collects a box full of tomatoes, and he goes up and down the block giving them away. I think he now has six neighbors who regularly get tomatoes from his vines. The people in four homes have refused to take any. I don't know why they don't—that's his and their problem, I guess. But I do know it hurts him, because he really wants to give.

Other acts could be added to this list. Such things as
cutting lawns
raking leaves
shoveling snow
helping a sexton clean a church for a special event
buying a nightgown for a newborn infant (one was for my own grandson)
shopping in the grocery store for a sick neighbor (in many situations such transactions are done by written note, since the person with the handicap may have trouble reading).

Lists like these will grow steadily from now on. Chances are, you yourself can now add to this list.

Such individualized giving reflects one more aspect of the public's refreshing change in attitude toward people with developmental disabilities. Now they can be free-hearted givers too. They will no longer suffer the cruel indignity of always having to take and never being able to give. And with this societal shift, you have a fresh opportunity to make clear, unashamed decisions about taking the gifts they bring, or saying no thanks. Then people with handicaps will achieve a healthy balance of give-and-take. And as you receive from them, you will also be giving—more than you ever have before.

We put all kinds of grocery items in the basket. Of course, there were many steps to this program, which I wrote down in my task analysis—getting the cart; putting cans in the bottom and things like bread and eggs on the top; discussing each item as it went into the basket; talking about which soap to use for dishes, clothes, and hair. Then after the basket was full, we put them back on the shelves. And as he got better and better at it, I faded and let him do the shopping tasks on his own.

That's how a Canadian student at St. Pierre Collegiate High School described her down-to-earth training program for a young man with mental retardation, who recently had moved into the community from an institution. However, as the student talked, my mind began to wonder about what other people in the market had been thinking. So I said, "How did the grocery store manager respond to what you were doing?" There was a pause. Then she said quietly, "I don't know. She didn't say anything. She didn't make any big deal out of it. Why? Should she have?"

Earlier, three St. Pierre students and three teen-agers with developmental disabilities had been eating together in a restaurant in St. Malo, when a drunken man left his table and walked over to theirs. In a loud voice he attacked the group. "Some of these people don't belong here—they need to be with their own kind!" Everyone sat calmly while the manager of the restaurant walked over and ordered the abusive man to leave. The man left. And everyone in the restaurant went right on eating as if nothing had happened. Again, one of the students stated, "It wasn't any big thing."

A hard-nosed review of the early material for this book, done by Richard and Dee Voorhees of Bloomington, Minnesota, came back into my consciousness after the interviews with those Canadians. The Voorhees were among many neighborhood people who thus far had had no immediate contact with persons having developmental disabilities. (Such reviewers saved you, the reader, from poring over hundreds of superfluous pages!)

[Said Richard Voorhees] I suspect pioneers in the movement need to make lots of noise every time they achieve some sort of new breakthrough. But I doubt if ordinary citizens will do what they do with as much fanfare. Neighbors will just go ahead and do it because a perceptual revolution toward such people has reached them, so that now they automatically do it, merely out of the goodness of their hearts.[1]

[Said Dee Voorhees] I think neighbors need to feel they are doing something very ordinary, very human, in being an ordinary friend and advocate, rather than being some sort of noble revolutionary.

Such interesting responses the neighbors are giving these days! And they are expressed in such a relaxed, easy manner, as
   no big deal
   no big thing
   no need to do what they do with as much fanfare
   merely doing something very ordinary, very human
   no noble revolutionaries
   no press releases
   no Sunday features
   no TV documentaries
   no special award plaques for outstanding services rendered
   something neighbors will be doing automatically
   something they will merely go ahead and do, out of the goodness of their hearts.

This is the way civilization betters itself: Change begins with highly visible revolutions but ends with unpretentious ones. In other words, *improvement in a society's attitude toward persons with handicaps will not be*

---

1. It was Richard Voorhees who called my attention to the concept of *perceptual revolution,* as described in Thomas S. Kuhn, *The Structure of Scientific Revolutions* (Chicago: The University of Chicago Press, 1962).

complete until the breakthroughs of its trailblazers—scientists, philosophers, educators, social servants, change agents, and committed volunteers—become second nature to ordinary citizens in ordinary neighborhoods. It started as a very big deal, but as the changes take place, most people will see them as no big deal at all. Acceptance of people with developmental disabilities will be so commonplace that we will only wonder why it took so long to come about.

• Twice in this century, key leaders and their movements have attempted to create a superrace by identifying and discarding persons with handicaps. And as some of us reflect on the Eugenic Movement of the early 1900s and the Holocaust of the late 1930s and early 1940s—with their utter repulsiveness and their miserable failure—we are developing the good sense to see that persons with handicaps figure as much as anyone else in society's advancement. This amounts to a beautiful reversal of society's attitude.

• There has to be more to life than merely trying to be better than the next person. For example, the camera focuses on a player or a spectator at a televised athletic event. The person, sensing that he or she is "on," often automatically raises the index finger and makes the we-are-number-one gesture. And many of us watching at home momentarily feel our stomachs turn. We are irritated by that oft-repeated, mindless gesture. And the same can be said for blind strivings

> to be in the "top ten"
> to be "above average"
> never to be seen as "below average" (although 50 percent of us are in that category, no matter which way the line is drawn).

Such vain competitions are now beginning to weary many of us. We would like to leave them behind, just as we left behind King of the Hill, a game we played as children, in which we struggled for the top by kicking and pushing others down.

• Not so long ago, *survival of the fittest* was seen by many as the single thrust that advances civilization. However, today it is perfectly clear that many who are striving to be the fittest are capable of blowing themselves and us off the face of the earth, in an attempt to prove that they are superior and the true elite. Now that we know this, we are rapidly becoming aware that, actually, *we all figure in one another's survival.*

• People were meant to complement each other. Where I am strong, you may be weak. At points where you excel, I may be all thumbs. And the ultimate tragedy takes place when I reject you because of your handicaps and you reject me because of mine. Then we live apart . . . and we die apart. We die without ever really *knowing* each other or experiencing the rich contributions each could have made to the other's life.

• The solving of individual differences in people adds creativity and zest to any society. Of course, such differences can cause fears and tensions, but as we work to diminish those fears, we often discover mutual appreciations, respects, and loves we have never before experienced. Also, we are learning that life is really at its downright dullest when everyone we know thinks and functions exactly as we do.

• Societies that are moving forward are also reaching back. For example, there is something deep within me that tells me *I must strive to reach forward and do the best I can with what I have, and I must reach back and help my brothers and sisters with their development, too.* It is my hunch that such an urge can be found somewhere within the depths of your being as well. If this notion is valid, then it is the proper *balancing* of our competitions and our cooperations that enables civilization to take an evolutionary leap forward.

The discoveries and skills learned in neighborhood settings, from mutually healthy relationships with people who have handicaps, will lead us to find a valuable new principle.

The more advanced a civilization becomes, the more it will understand, value, and relate healthily to its members who have severe handicapping conditions.

Epilogue

This book has ended.

It has been an attempt to fashion a pair of prescription lenses for you; to provide an opportunity for you to see persons with developmental disabilities more clearly than you have seen them before. You may be interested in knowing that when this manuscript was first written, it contained four times as many words as it now does. But you do not need heavy binoculars or a microscope. You need only simple, ordinary, corrective glasses, which will enable you to appreciate the people with handicaps who soon will be

> living in ordinary houses and apartments like yours;
>
> passing you or standing next to you on the streets;
>
> riding with you on buses, trolleys, and subways;
>
> rubbing elbows with you in shopping centers;
>
> going to public school with the other kids on the block;
>
> working in the same building where you work;
>
> making money and paying taxes;
>
> seen in restaurants, theaters, and at athletic events;
>
> sitting beside you in churches and synagogues.

And when people are living that close to you, it is a pity if old myths and fears continue to fog your vision so that you see them only as blurred oblong figures . . . and fail to recognize the remarkable personalities, faiths, strengths, loves, and loyalties that these people often possess.

But *seeing* them as they really are and *knowing* them in real face-to-face encounters are two different things. This book can only help you with the first step. You, yourself, must choose to take the second!

Some of the best friends I have can neither read or write. But the many things they have been able to do with me and for me have outweighed many times the things they could not do. And my relationships with such people have been so rich that my world-view has changed for the better. Over the years, they have introduced me to a world I had never known before. And as bewildering as it seems, it is a world that society had programmed me to shun and stay away from. But I didn't stay away. And I'm glad I didn't!

I wonder if you feel as I do . . . or if someday you will. . . .

PERSKE '79